Deviance: A Cross-Cultural Perspective

Deviance: A Cross-Cultural Perspective

Robert B. Edgerton
University of California, Los Angeles

Cummings Publishing Company
Menlo Park, California · Reading, Massachusetts
London · Amsterdam · Don Mills, Ontario · Sydney

This book is in the
Cummings Modular Program in Anthropology

This work is based in part on material in the module entitled
Deviant Behavior and Cultural Theory, © 1973 by Addison-Wesley Publishing Company, Inc.

Library of Congress Catalog Card No. 75-28641

ISBN-0-8465-1301-3 Paperbound Edition
ISBN-0-8465-1300-5 Clothbound Edition
ABCDEFGHIJKL—AL—79876

Cummings Publishing Company, Inc.
2727 Sand Hill Road
Menlo Park, California 94025

Contents

To my parents

About the Author

Robert B. Edgerton is a Professor of Anthropology in the Departments of Psychiatry and Anthropology, University of California, Los Angeles, where he has taught since 1962. He has conducted fieldwork with the Menomini Indians of Wisconsin, four societies in East Africa, Polynesian Hawaiians, and various urban populations in the United States. In addition to deviant behavior, his major interests include mental retardation and theories of incompetence, mental illness, and various aspects of psychological anthropology. His earlier books include *The Cloak of Competence, Changing Perspectives in Mental Illness* (with S. Plog), *Drunken Comportment* (with C. MacAndrew), *The Individual in Cultural Adaptation*, and *Methods and Styles in the Study of Culture* (with L. L. Langness).

Acknowledgments

I would like to thank C. M. Edgerton, P. S. Hartmann, and L. L. Langness for commenting on various versions of this manuscript. I also wish to thank Jae Stewart for seeing the manuscript through its many versions. I wish to acknowledge support from the University of California, and Grant No. HD-04612, Mental Retardation Research Center, University of California, Los Angeles. To the many students who have commented on this material in an earlier form, I offer my special thanks.

Introduction

There are people in all societies who steal, murder, rape, cheat, lie, betray, bully, blaspheme, or otherwise offend. Such people make trouble for other people who then react with indignation, outrage, horror, or direct punitive action. People who make trouble for others by breaking socially accepted rules are known in the social sciences as *deviants*. In everyday life, deviance is a practical problem influenced by law or custom or decency and it requires practical solutions. For social scientists, the problems raised by deviance are theoretical. Why do some people, and not others, break rules and cause trouble? What happens to them when they do? In seeking the answers to these important yet unanswered questions, we shall find that the most fundamental issues about man and society must also be raised.

We shall begin with a summary of the prevailing theory concerning deviant behavior and a brief review of the history of competing theories and ideas. Next, we shall consider the most common social, cultural, psychological, and biological explanations of deviant behavior. We shall then review various kinds of deviant behavior that occur in the world's smaller and simpler societies. This review will illustrate many of the problems that now exist in conceptualizing and explaining deviance. Finally, the evidence will be reviewed, the explanations evaluated, and we will conclude with a discussion of the fundamental role of the concept of human nature, not only for an understanding of deviant behavior, but for an understanding of society itself.

More specifically, we shall introduce and challenge the conventional point of view concerning the causes of deviant behavior, relying primarily on evidence from "folk" societies. In so doing we shall evaluate various theories that compare deviance in folk and urban societies. We shall suggest that conventional views of deviant behavior have been limited by their common failure to utilize relevant biological perspectives, and we shall also point to the necessity of distinguishing deviant persons from deviant acts.

Chapter 1

Background to the Cross-Cultural Study of Deviance

It is a safe assumption that there are few among us who have not done something of consequence which we knew was wrong—we may have regretted doing what we did, but we did it nonetheless. What is more, there cannot be many among us who can honestly say that they will never do anything wrong again. But some among us misbehave and cause trouble more often than others. So it is in the Ituri Forest, the Kalahari Desert, the islands of the Pacific, the forests of South America and the shores of Alaska. While social scientists recognize that wrongdoing occurs everywhere, they also assume that it is usually relatively infrequent; conformity and troublefree behavior are agreed to be both typical and natural. Thus, conformity—people behaving as their cultural rules would have them behave—has been recognized by virtually everyone in social science as the dominant fact of life everywhere.

The sociologist, Dennis Wrong (1961), has called this prevailing belief the conventional wisdom, referring to it as the "oversocialized view of man," because it assumes that man is easily socialized to do what is expected of him. In this conventional view it is assumed that man wants to behave correctly for two reasons: (1) because he internalizes his culture, and (2) because he seeks the esteem of his

3

fellow men.   These two sovereign mechanisms have been
used to explain—to the complete satisfaction of many—
why conformity and social order come to pass.   Therefore, it has been thought unnecessary to ask why
social order exists.   The answer is obvious.   We know
why people usually conform; what we need to ask is why
they sometimes deviate.   That man "naturally" conforms
is the conventional wisdom.   It is important to understand how it arises.

We can begin with Thomas Hobbes, whose concern
with the origins of social order has become famous as
the "Hobbesian problem of order."   Born in 1588—the
year that the Spanish Armada was defeated—he lived
his 91 years in the turbulent 17th century, a fact
which no doubt shaped his view of man and his problems.   He is known for his reported view that the
natural condition of man is "the war of all men
against all men."   For Hobbes this condition had never
actually existed but was only an analytical concept
useful in understanding what man would be like were it
not for the restraints of reason or society.   Hobbes
felt that man's nature was such that if each man were
left free to pursue his own self-interest, the result
would not always be cooperation and exchange.   Collu-
sion, force, and fraud would also present themselves
as rationally attractive alternatives.   For Hobbes,
then, it was natural for people to pursue their own
self-interest, and to do so by deviant means if necessary.   Hobbes' solution was to control man's deviance
by giving the state—the Leviathan as he referred to
it—a monopoly over the legitimate use of force in the
maintenance of order.   John Locke, a young contemporary
of Hobbes, disagreed saying that social order was not
to be achieved by force but depended instead upon a
broad stratum of common values and interests, a
"natural identity of interests" as he put it.   Locke
took the existence of such shared interests for granted, as if they were given in man's nature.   In Locke's
terms, if left alone, man would not war against other
men; he would cooperate.

The Hobbesian view that only force prevented man from expressing the dark side of his nature found some support in the Church, where earthly authority and divinity alike were seen to be in a constant struggle with man's sinfulness and with satanic forces in the universe. We might note, for example, that St. Paul's theory of man's evil nature—often favored by the Church—was more extreme than Hobbes' own. Hobbes actually came closer to Aristotle, who saw man as both beast *and* angel. Among modern scholars, the theory most compatible with Hobbes was probably Freud's, arguing as it did for a human "id" bursting with sexual energy and innate aggression against which the "ego" and "superego" must struggle for control. Views of human nature as evil were not uncommon among turn-of-the-century sociologists. One of the greatest of these, Georg Simmel, believed that man had an *"a priori* fighting instinct," and Simmel did Hobbes one better as an aphorist with his *homo homini lupus* (man is wolf to man).

In time, Locke's perspective gained many more converts than did Hobbes' more dismal ideas. Among the most important in swinging the tide against Hobbes was the French sociologist, Emile Durkheim, who, writing at the time of Simmel, insisted that man *wants* to be "moral." In Durkheim's view, man receives positive satisfaction from conforming; virtue is indeed its own reward. Yet Durkheim also saw that deviance was inevitable. Durkheim imagined a society of perfect saints where crimes, as other men know them, would never occur. But faults that would be trivial for ordinary men would create scandal for the saints. As Sartre (1964) put it years later, "To give oneself laws and to create the possibility of disobeying them come to the same thing." The idea that society—not man's animal instincts—is the source of deviance still occupies center stage in modern social science. Another idea of Durkheim's was less well received. In 1895 Durkheim wrote that crime was "an integral part of all healthy societies," because its occurrence draws people together in common anger and indignation (Durkheim 1938, translation). Recently, sociologist

Kai Erikson (1966) has attempted to apply Durkheim's
idea to Puritan deviance but in general, the notion
that deviance is either natural to man or necessary
for social health has not been widely accepted. Although other influences were also at work in bringing
about a shift away from Hobbes (instinct theory, for
example, which might have focused attention on man's
deviant nature, was dying at the hands of overzealous
psychologists who made ludicrous overstatements),
none was more instrumental than sociological theory
built upon Durkheim's foundation.

In American sociology, the most important theory
relating to the problem of deviance and order was
developed by Talcott Parsons, beginning in the 1930's.
Expressed in a number of articles and books and carried throughout the academic world by Parsons' influential students from Harvard, the theory purported to
solve the Hobbesian problem of the origins of social
order. Parsons admitted that external force, as seen
by Hobbes, was an important source of order, but he
placed it in a secondary position to Locke's shared
values. He also invoked *social equilibrium* as an
additional important concept. Parsons believed that
individuals in a social system *do* share values (norms,
or rules if you wish) and that people tend to act in
accordance with them. The resulting regular patterns
of behavior can be thought of as a structure. This
structure is in equilibrium—a delicate and self-cor-
recting balance.

This equilibrium is maintained by two phenomena.
First, and most important, is socialization, the
process by which children learn to do, and learn to
want to do, what is required and expected by others.
The principal mechanism in this process is *the desire
for approval*. The results of the process of socialization are often unconscious to that people "internal-
ize" values and motives, thus reaffirming Durkheim's
insight that people *feel* rewarded when they behave as
they should. Second, should socialization not suffice
to keep people in line, there is social control, both
external, as Hobbes had in mind, and internal, as

Freud presented it when he saw guilt as a basic factor in the development of "civilization."

Parsons' so-called functionalist position ruled
sociology for over three decades before it came under
serious attack. This is particularly remarkable for
several reasons. First, there was Parsons' labyrin-
thine and inflated style of writing. More serious
was the failure of his theory to account for the occurrence of deviance except as a consequence of
social disequilibrium. The sociology of sociology
necessary to account for the prolonged, and continuing, success of Parsonian "functionalism" is beyond
the scope of our concern. Alvin Gouldner's *The Coming
Crisis of Western Sociology* (1970) introduces this
subject with elegance and significance. It is enough
here to note that the study of "social deviance" has
been greatly influenced by Parsons. As a result, for
American sociology, and for social science in general,
deviance has not been looked upon as a product of
man's nature; it has been seen consistently as the
result of a disturbance in social equilibrium.

If sociologists typically ignored man's nature
or his personal pathology as causes of deviance,
psychologists and psychiatrists did not, often locating the cause of man's misbehavior in his psychopathology or his basic animal nature. However, over the
years that followed Freud, the source of deviant
behavior came to be found less and less in man's
nature, and more and more in his social and cultural
environment. This *environmentalist* perspective has
come to dominate even in psychoanalysis. Thus, for
example, Judd Marmor, writing in *Modern Psychoanalysis*, (1968, p. 4) says: "In advanced psychoanalytic
circles today the focus of psychopathology is no
longer being sought—at least to the same degree as
formerly—within the individual's psyche, but rather
in his system of relationships, his family, his
small groups, his community, his society." We shall
return to the question of how well this point of
view has explained the puzzling presence of deviance
in man's societies. For the moment, however, it is

sufficient to note that throughout the social and
psychological sciences the primary cause of deviance
has been thought to be in man's social and cultural
environment, not in man himself, and that the frequency of deviance has consistently been "underesti-
mated" (Matza, 1969).

The role of anthropology in the development of
this conventional perspective on man's deviance has
been indirect, but important. It has been indirect
in the sense that, unlike sociologists and psychologists, anthropologists have written very little
about "deviant behavior"; it has been important,
nonetheless, because what anthropologists have written about culture and human deviance has been most
influential. This influence begins with the study of
culture. That human behavior is highly patterned,
that it reflects "culture," is a major contribution
of anthropology. This discovery was given even
greater force by the realization that people everywhere not only follow cultural rules, but that these
rules often seem to be arbitrary, varying as they do
so dramatically from one society to the next. Anthropologists have again and again reported the diverse and arbitrary nature of man's rules about dress,
food, sex, religion, etiquette, marriage, politics,
and the like. They have also reported that people
cherish these seemingly arbitrary rules, live by
them, and are sometimes willing to die for them. If
cultural rules are so varied, and if people in all
societies learn to follow these rules, then the conclusion seems to follow that man is a highly social
and malleable creature, willing and able to live within the rules of any society, however bizarre these
rules might seem to outsiders.

The concept of human plasticity rests upon the
notion of *tabula rasa*, the idea that a human being
is born without instincts and is totally the product
of his experience. The term is John Locke's, but it
was stated even more forcefully by Montesquieu and
later given powerful support by John Dewey. The
idea has probably received its greatest force from

anthropologists. Although the *tabula rasa* concept is likely to be disavowed today whenever it becomes explicit, the following *tabula rasa* assumption has nevertheless been implicitly accepted throughout social science: human infants are born sufficiently plastic that they can easily learn to live in any "normally functioning" society. For most, an even stronger *tabula rasa* assumption is made: man is so plastic that he has *no* nature. These assumptions lead to the conclusion that should people come to deviate, as they do from time to time, the fault must lie in the disequilibrium of society, not in the people themselves.

These and related assumptions have their roots deep in anthropological history. Early in this century, Franz Boas, his many prominent students, and other anthropologists were dedicated to showing the equality of races and of cultures. This was done by attacking the earlier notions that race was somehow tied to culture and showing instead that there was no relationship whatsoever between race and culture. Moreover, human nature—what all races share as their biological inheritance—became equally insignificant, being seen almost solely as a product of culture, not biology. Margaret Mead described the temper of those times in this manner:

> It was a simple—a very simple—point to which our materials were organized in the 1920's, merely the documentation over and over of the fact that human nature is not rigid and unyielding . . . but . . . extraordinarily adaptable. (1939, p. x)

This battle against human nature was successful, and culture was accorded a dominant position in the study of man:

> The battle which we once had to fight with the whole battery at our command, with the most fantastic and startling examples that we could muster, is now won. (Mead, 1939, pp. x-xi)

Another important influence was the configuration theory of Ruth Benedict. Presenting her thesis in several articles as well as in her immensely popular book, *Patterns of Culture* (1934), she made explicit a position which had great impact in other fields and which, despite criticism, has also had a lasting influence in anthropology. Her theory may be summarized in the following terms: first, in every culture, infants are born with a wide range of individual temperament types (genetically and constitutionally determined). However, every culture permits only a limited number of these types to flourish, and they are those that fit its dominant configuration. "Fortunately," the "vast majority" of individuals in any society will be able to conform to the dominant type of that society, since most temperaments will be sufficiently plastic to be molded by the force of the society. Those few who cannot be molded will be deviants.

Despite interest in Benedict's theory and in "abnormality," anthropology was slow to study the process of becoming deviant. For example, interest in *abnormality* sometimes led to interesting findings related to deviance, but most of these studies had to do with presumed psychopathology (of psychotics, shamans, homosexuals, etc.), or with the idea that customs which were *normal* in one society could be *abnormal* in another. The process by which someone came to be regarded as deviant was only rarely touched upon. Instead, anthropology concentrated upon the processes by which the vast majority was molded during socialization. Only rarely was there concern with rule violation or with troublemaking as such, either in the process of socialization or in the adult "personalities" that emerged from it. There was an occasional report that related to deviance, often from Rorschach testing of an aberrant individual, but it was not until the *modal personality* studies of the 1950's that it became clear how much the earlier focus of the "culture and personality" period on typical persons had served to obscure both individual diversity and deviance (Singer, 1961). But even these more recent studies, despite their emphasis on

individual variation, say little or nothing about deviant behavior. Until quite recently, when data relevant to deviance were reported by anthropologists,
it was typically found under such headings as "conflict," "social control," or "law," and while much of
this material was of high quality it had little impact
upon the prevailing understanding of deviant behavior,
either in anthropology or in the other social sciences.

As for the study of deviant individuals—those who
were *not* molded—the pickings were also slim. Margaret
Mead wrote as much about such persons as anyone, both
on Samoa and in New Guinea, but even her work reflected the configurational pattern of Benedict. We learned
a great deal about what was typical and customary but
only relatively little about a man or woman who was
one of a very few members of his or her society who
did not fit. Information about such persons was often
set aside in an isolated chapter or an appendix (some
of the work of George Devereux (1961) is an exception). We also learned of a few deviants in American
Indian societies—the Hopi, Sun Chief; the Winnebago,
Crashing Thunder; or the Navajo hand trembler, Gre-
gorio. Such accounts, when they were written at all,
were typically in the form of life histories (Langness, 1965). Accounts of how men conducted their
everyday affairs, including deviance, and how they
dealt with those among them who "deviated," were
rare indeed. We were told mostly about a few conspicuous deviants, and in the absence of information
about less extreme deviance or everyday misbehavior,
many readers came to the conclusion that Benedict was
right: a few people cannot be molded and these are
obvious deviants; the rest live troublefree lives
within the rules of their culture.

Although anthropologists have always recognized
that "primitive" men do express individuality, they
have usually *written* as if this knowledge were of
little theoretical importance (Goodman, 1967). Perhaps as a consequence, many social scientists outside
of anthropology believe primitive men to be truly the
slaves of custom, or as Yehudi Cohen once put it, that

they are the men in the grey flannel loin-cloths.
However unintentional, anthropology perpetuated this
belief by many of its practices. Often, when anthropologists wrote about the life of a non-Western people,
they generalized to such a degree that individual variability was lost in the search for patterns, regularities, or typical behaviors. Since anthropologists
were in the business of searching for regularities of
behavior—culture—they not only often failed to record
variability, they sometimes even failed to see it when
it was right before their eyes. Moreover, when they
attempted to make theoretical sense out of cultural
materials, they often failed to make reference to dis-
crepant beliefs, deviant behaviors and organizational
anomalies. Such discrepancies, anomalies, and deviance were simply not the problem at hand, and most
anthropologists have learned to correct for the absence of these considerations when they read about
another society. But the theory of deviance was developed in sociology and psychology, and theorists in
these fields were unlikely to know what anthropologists left out.

In the last decade or so anthropological practices
of field research, the problems anthropologists study,
and the ways in which they report their data have
changed (see, for example, the February 1975, Special
Issue of the *American Ethnologist* which is entirely
devoted to intra-cultural variation), but the practices of earlier decades have helped to create general
and often implicit theories of man and society, especially in other social sciences. Theories change
slowly, and implicit ones change slower still. One
such implicit theory, which has to do with differences
between *folk* and *urban* populations, has had enormous
influence upon the study of deviant behavior. This
theory is important, pervasive, and often taken for
granted. The theory was given its greatest thrust in
anthropology by Robert Redfield (1947) in his well-
known folk-urban typology. For Redfield, a folk
society is small, homogeneous, non-literate, isolated,
and displays a strong sense of community. Such a

society is almost entirely free of deviance or disruption. In contrast, urban society is characterized by heterogeneity, deviance, and disorder. Despite recent erosion of some of its underpinnings, this distinction between folk and urban ways of life is very much a part of modern anthropology, and of social science in general. In fact, the ideas embodied in the shift from folk *community* to urban *society* have been among the most fundamental and widely used in all of social science (Mills, 1950).

As the Spanish historian, Julio Caro Baroja (1963), has pointed out, the folk-urban distinction is ancient, being prominent in the works of Aristophanes and Tacitus, not to mention the Old Testament where it receives particular emphasis with the rural life being not only good and noble, but divine as well, and the city life epitomizing man's evil. The folk-urban comparison has achieved intellectual prominence, however, through a series of formulations by 19th century scholars. There were many precursors, of course, including Karl Marx and W. H. Morgan, but the idea was given particularly cogent and explicit form by Ferdinand Tönnies who, as a young man of 32, wrote *Gemeinschaft und Gesellschaft* in 1887 in which he compared folk with urban social forms.

Tönnies drew from at least three significant prior works. Henry Maine, an English jurist, wrote *Ancient Law* in 1861 and in it he stressed the evolution from communities based on *status* to those based on *contract*. In 1864, Fustel de Coulanges wrote *The Ancient City*. He compared the stable, closed communities of earliest Athens and Rome with the open individualized communities that each place later became. In 1868 Otto von Gierke wrote his monumental *Das Deutsche Genossenschaftsrecht*. At the center of his thinking was the vivid contrast between the medieval social structure with its organic unity of all communal and corporate groups before the law, and the modern nation-state with its centralization of political power and its liberation of the individual.

We should keep in mind that these men wrote at a
time when European industrial growth was not only
transforming community life, but was creating large
populations where before only villages had existed.
Manchester, England, for example, grew from 20,000 in
1750 to an industrial center of 142,000 in 1831 (Fried-
rich Engels' Marxian writings were based upon his
experiences in Manchester). Such cities were taking
on a decidely unlovely aspect as John Ruskin vividly
tells us in his view of London, written in 1865:
"That great foul city—rattling, growling, smoking,
stinking—a ghastly heap of fermenting brickwork,
pouring out poison at every pore." Tönnies' work, then,
was both an elaboration of what had been written before and a reaction to changes that were so visibly
taking place in Europe.

Tönnies' formulation was followed by complemen-
tary versions by such important scholars as Georg
Simmel, Emile Durkheim, Herbert Spencer, Max Weber,
Robert MacIver, Charles Cooley, and Howard Becker.
As the sociologist Robert Nisbet (1966) has said, the
fundamental issue in all of these positions is the
loss of *community*. The folk society was said to be
epitomized by "community" as constituted by personal
intimacy, emotional depth, moral commitment, social
cohesion and continuity in time. In the transition
to urban society it was thought that each of these
was lost. As Disraeli once put it: "In great cities
men are brought together by the desire to gain. They
are not in a state of cooperation but isolation . . .
modern society acknowledges no neighbor."

The same comparison became important in anthropology in the late 1940's when Robert Redfield wrote
"The Folk Society" (1947). Redfield's idea was
developed in subsequent articles and books, and its
impact has been long-lasting (Goodman, 1967). Some
anthropologists continue to restate the same basic
folk-urban theory in their own terms, as for example,
in the folk-like "personal community" of Jules Henry
(1958). Others merely reflect these ideas in their
thinking and writing. In many respects, these anthropological folk-urban comparisons only repeated the

folk-urban distinctions of earlier scholars. But in
another respect they went beyond these earlier views,
in that unlike the earlier theories which were derived primarily from Western experience, these anthropological theories were based upon knowledge of societies throughout the world. The theories are important
for this discussion because they provided additional
confirmation that folk societies were, as Benedict had
said, largely free of deviants. They were places
where custom ruled, few people caused trouble, and
those who did became highly visible "deviants."

   While the folk-urban comparison continues to exert
its influence, there has long been an accumulation of
contrary evidence. For example, we can now see that
even the most dedicated believers in the folk society
did not provide as convincing a portrait as they had
thought. The ideal of the folk society was stated
perfectly by Jane Belo, as she wrote some years ago
about the island of Bali: "The babies do not cry, the
small boys do not fight, the young girls bear themselves with decorum . . . Everyone carries out his
appointed task, with respect for his equals and supe-
riors, and gentleness and consideration for his depen-
dents. The people adhere, apparently with ease, to
the laws governing the actions, big and small, of their
lives" (1935, p. 141). Unfortunately for those who
would like to take this idyllic vision to heart, Belo
went on, unwittingly one presumes, to document contrary instances in which men beat their wives, wives
berated husbands and ran away from home, children
quarreled with their parents, and men and women alike
rebelled against the constraints of Balinese custom
and authority.

   Benedict's own account of the Zuni Indians was
similarly challenged, although by other anthropologists rather than her own contradictory material. In
Patterns of Culture, Benedict reported that, unlike
most other American Indians, the Zuni did not have a
problem with alcohol (1934, p. 82): "Drunkenness is
repulsive to them. In Zuni after the early introduction of liquor, the old men voluntarily outlawed it

and the rule was congenial enough to be honored."
Other observers, including novelist Edmund Wilson,
told a different story, finding widespread drunkenness among the Zuni. For example, Smith and Roberts
(1954) reported that in 1949, the most common "crimes"
in Zuni were drunkenness and drunken driving. Had so
much changed in 15 years or had Benedict provided an
idealized account of a deviance-free folk society?
Anthropologists today generally agree that her report
was idealized.

Oscar Lewis, Redfield's former student, raised
further questions when his study of the Mexican town
of Tepoztlan did not accord with Redfield's earlier
account of the same town. Redfield's study of Tepoztlan had emphasized its tranquil, contented people
living a life of almost ideal social integration and
individual adjustment. Lewis (1951), on the other
hand, convincingly reported widespread social conflict along with a high level of gossip, mistrust,
hatred, and fear. This disagreement was particularly
jarring since it was from his study of Tepoztlan that
Redfield drew much of the background for his conception of the folk society.

Similar doubts were raised by the anthropologist
John Bennett who noted the "general critical attitude
of the social scientist toward the heterogeneity of
modern life, and a fairly clear attitude toward the
organic character of preliterate life as preferable"
(1956, p. 205). The bias Bennett noted has also
been seen by others; for example, John Madge (1962)
accused prominent sociologists concerned with social
deviance of bias in idealizing the "village" against
which their urban communities were unfavorably compared, and by historians Carl Schorske and Oscar
Handlin who have discussed the varying views of the
city in European thought. As Morton and Lucia White
(1962) have shown in *The Intellectual Versus the
City*, American intellectuals have consistently
thought of the city as a place of evil and pathology.

Despite criticisms such as these, many social
scientists, including anthropologists, continue to

accept the fundamental premise of the folk-urban distinction that deviance is rare in folk societies. This premise follows logically from the established beliefs about man and socialization that we have discussed. Thus, if man is malleable and is willingly and easily socialized, then small, isolated, well-integrated societies should more or less effortlessly succeed in molding their members into good citizens, leaving very few who become deviants. But as societies grow, diversify, and change, socialization should be less successful and deviance should increase. Logically, all this follows. The evidence, of course, is something else again.

The folk-urban distinction is part of a theory of human behavior and deviance that has grown to a position of prominence. Anthropology played a role in the development of this theory, as did other sciences. If this theory is to receive systematic evaluation, however, anthropology must play a major role, for anthropologists are best equipped to gather and evaluate evidence about deviant behavior in folk societies. After introducing the various explanations of deviant behavior that are currently employed, some illustrations of deviant behavior in folk societies will be presented. We shall then reconsider the adequacy of the folk-urban distinction as well as the more general theory of human behavior and deviance of which it is a part.

Chapter 2
Explanations of Deviance

Why do people deviate? Why do they break their societies' rules, straying from the path that most people
follow? As sociologist A. K. Cohen (1966, p. 41) has
put it, there are as many ways of explaining misbehavior as there are ways of misbehaving, and there
are innumerable ways of misbehaving. Indeed, the task
of creating theories to explain man's deviance has
stood as one of the most difficult challenges for all
the sciences of human behavior. Our currently available explanations of deviance are as yet partial,
unconnected and conflicting, but they can be classi-
fied. Speaking generally, there are five classes of
explanations of deviance commonly in use in the social
or behavioral sciences: (1) social strain, (2) sub-
cultural conflict, (3) psychological defense or commitment, (4) biological defect, and, (5) human nature.
There are also *accounts*, that is explanations offered
by the participants themselves. Needless to say,
these classes of explanations are actually used in
many modifications and combinations. Yet, because
each class of explanation makes somewhat different
assumptions, it is useful to deal with each one separately. The reason for discussing these explanations
is not to examine the many complexities relating to
any form of explanation in the social sciences, but
rather to illustrate the theories and assumptions that
are most important in the study of deviant behavior.

SOCIAL STRAIN

This position originated with Durkheim and received its foremost expression from the sociologist, Robert Merton. It is a prominent, perhaps even dominant, notion in sociology and it fits well with the conventional wisdom. Social strain (or anomie) theory assumes that man is a highly moral creature who not only respects the rules of his society but internalizes them so that deviance is very unlikely, perhaps even unthinkable under normal conditions. Given this assumption that man *wants* to conform, the cause of deviance is found to lie in some major dislocation of the social fabric, a dislocation by which man is "frustrated," "alienated," "deprived," "discontented," or "anomic." More specifically, man will deviate from the expectations of his fellow men only if he experiences some major disjunction between his *goals* and the legitimate *means* of attaining them, or if the rules themselves become contradictory or meaningless.

This explanation of deviance focuses not on the characteristics of individuals, but on the positions that individuals occupy in the social system. It is a sociological approach. Furthermore, it makes it possible to talk about both conformity and the several varieties of deviance in terms of a simple and parsimonious conceptual scheme—i.e., means and goals. The theory of social strain, or anomie, has been widely applied, especially in the study of urban crime and delinquency. The basic ideas of social strain theory have been virtually taken for granted. For example, the important "Chicago school" of social deviance made *social disorganization* its central concept for explaining deviance (Matza, 1969, p. 45). In doing so they created an idealized vision of the deviance-free *organization* they presumed to exist in folk communities, which they contrasted with the deviant behavior they studied in urban neighborhoods. Similar views have become important in many fields, as for example, in the definition of mental illness used by the influential Cornell-Aro project of Alexander

Leighton and his colleagues. *Social integration* is presumed to be the natural or *folk* way, and these integrated societies are said to lack conflict, deviance and mental illness. *Disintegrated* societies, on the other hand, are *defined* by the presence of conflict, deviance, and mental illness (see Kaplan, 1971). This means that the basic assumption of social strain theory is simply accepted, not critically examined. If a society has a high rate of deviance it *must* be undergoing social strain; if a society has a low rate of deviance, then by definition, it suffers little social strain. The assumptions of the folk-urban comparison are obviously part and parcel of social strain or anomie theories.

Social strain theory has been influential and continues to serve many social scientists as the best available explanation for various kinds of deviance, especially the deviance displayed by the urban lower classes who aspire to middle-class goals but who are unable to attain them. This kind of theory is often used in combination with others, as for example, in the Watts Riots of 1965 where social strain—sometimes referred to as "relative deprivation"—was commonly linked with racism to explain an outbreak of violence and looting.

SUB-CULTURAL CONFLICT

The sub-cultural conflict explanation of deviance typically takes this form: people violate the rules of a society because the very act of conforming with their own way of life forces them into conflict with the culture of the dominant society. This perspective assumes that men do not, in fact, commit deviant acts. They act in accord with the expectations of their *own* reference group, but given the cultural pluralism of our modern nations, particularly the urban centers, one sub-culture's values may easily differ from and conflict with another's. The dominant political group may come to define the

behavior of subordinate groups as deviant. Also known
as the theory of "differential association" as proposed
by Edwin Sutherland and developed by Sutherland and
Cressey (1960), this theory has been widely employed to
explain juvenile gang delinquency or criminality by
showing how delinquent or criminal behaviors are
learned in interaction or "association" with members
of a reference group (an "intimate personal group,"
in Sutherland's words). A young man in a black ghetto
joins a street gang as his older brothers have done
before him, and a college student follows his culture
by smoking marijuana, just as a tribal African follows
his reference group in killing a witch. All may come
into conflict with the law of the larger society.

Sub-cultural conflict theory is frequently used
in combination with other theories. One such use, by
Cloward and Ohlin (1960), has achieved particular
prominence. Cloward and Ohlin have added the concept
of illegitimate opportunity to Merton's emphasis upon
goals and means. They note that sub-cultures differ
in their access to opportunity—both legitimate and
illegitimate. People with low access to legitimate
opportunity will feel social strain; those whose sub-
culture has high access to illegitimate opportunity
may learn to deviate. People with access to both may
have two pushes toward deviance. Thus, social strain
theory (conflict between goals and means) is combined with a version of sub-cultural theory (differential access to an opportunity structure).

PSYCHOLOGICAL DEFENSE OR COMMITMENT

Psychological explanations of deviance are diverse
and complex, falling into many classes. Four of
these classes have been used extensively. First,
there is the generalized idea of the *psychopath*,
or sociopath, someone who inherently lacks a concern
for morality and his fellow men. Such people are able
to commit ghastly crimes without any sense of remorse
or guilt. Freud (1930) originally noted that such
persons were numerous and could be constrained solely

by fear of punishment (as Hobbes had it, by the Leviathan) since moral constraint had no effect. Talcott Parsons invoked the same idea to account for the annoying presence of deviance but Parsons added a sense of irresistible impulse, saying that some men are not only psychopaths who lack any moral constraint, but possess as well a compelling need to deviate. Such men will find an outlet for their need to deviate by seeking an outlet within the constraints that society throws up around them. Whether psychopaths are born or made is still a matter of considerable disagreement.

Others have pointed to *early experience* as creating psychological tendencies to deviate. Many have used a psychodynamic perspective, while others have preferred social learning theory (Bandura and Walters, 1963). These theories, like sub-cultural ones, say that men learn to be deviant. They differ, however, by pointing to the individualized, unique learning experiences that lead to deviance, and by pointing out that such persons develop a psychological "need" (sometimes unconscious) to behave as they do. Thus, where a sub-cultural explanation would refer to the *shared* experiences of, let us say, Gypsies, that might lead them to steal from non-Gypsies, the early experience explanation refers to the unique (or at least uncommon) relationship of a boy to his father that later leads to the boy's deviance. For example, even Adolf Hitler's uniquely horrifying acts have been attributed to his incurable devotion to his mother, whom he allegedly idolized in so extreme a form that all other persons would be found unworthy (Payne, 1973).

A third psychological explanation sees deviance as a *reaction formation*—a defense that rejects something unacceptable or dangerous to the self by developing attitudes and behaviors that are apparently opposite. Thus, because many persons cannot succeed within the existing social system, and because this failure is painful to them, they reject the system with destructive nihilistic deviance (Cohen, 1966, pp. 65-66).

A final and quite different approach—*labeling*—
has been developed by the so-called "neo-Chicago"
school in sociology. Although this position was developed by sociologists (principal among whom are
Edwin Lemert, Howard Becker, and Erving Goffman), the
theory is nevertheless largely psychological. Lemert
coined the term "secondary deviation" to refer to the
process by which a person who has been labeled a
deviant (usually for a troublemaking act referred to
as "primary deviance") comes to employ additional acts
of deviance as a defense against, an attack upon or a
fulfillment of society's label. People who are labeled deviant may or may not accept this label but
their behavior is necessarily influenced by it. In
labeling theory, it is not the primary act of deviance that sets men apart. Many men occasionally
deviate. It is only when this act is discovered and
labeled deviant and a man's life becomes organized
around a conception of self as deviant, that he is
set apart and *becomes* deviant (Schur, 1971).

BIOLOGICAL DEFECT

There are also biological explanations of why people
sometimes perform deviant, or "anti-social" acts.
These kinds of answers were long in disrepute, taking
the form of "bad seed" or "criminal mind" explanations as popularized by Lombroso and Hooten. In
recent years, however, we have witnessed the increasing legitimization of answers that point to faulty
genetics (Rosenthal, 1971), improper nutrition (Birch
and Gussow, 1970), or birth traumata (Windle, 1969;
Mednick, 1970) as possible sources of deviant behavior. As we shall see later, studies linking temperament to deviance have achieved considerable scientific
acceptance (Escalona, 1968; Thomas *et al*, 1968).
Additional linkages of biology to deviance, such as
hormones to homosexuality (Green, 1973), genetics to
mental illness (Slater and Cowie, 1971), and brain
damage to aggression (Mark and Ervin, 1970) continue
to be developed. These kinds of explanations grow
in frequency, and probably in legitimacy, every day.

Such explanations may serve very well for some kinds
of deviance, as for example, certain types of mental
illness and mental retardation. But it should be emphasized that explanations which depend upon biological anomalies can hardly be expected to account for
more than a small percentage of the many cases of
treachery, theft, sexual misconduct, disbelief, violence, and other kinds of deviance that can occur in
any social system, unless it is assumed that almost
everyone has a significant biological defect. Only
if deviance is rare can theories of biological defect
take a prominent role in explaining deviant behavior.
    We should also note that theories which point to
defective biology are often called "control" theories.
They assume that some men deviate because they have a
biological predisposition to do so. Control theories,
therefore, look toward the development of techniques
of social or psychological control to keep such
deviance within acceptable bounds.

HUMAN NATURE

The final explanation assumes that human beings are
as naturally given to deviance as they are to conformity. This view follows more or less directly
from Hobbes who saw humans as potential deviants who
were best controlled by fear. In this view, the
achievement of social order is not a direct reflec-
tion of human nature; instead it becomes a social
responsibility necessary in order to control men who
would otherwise be engaged, at least part of the
time, in the "war of all against all." Therefore,
deviance is seen as being perfectly natural; it is
social order that must be accounted for.
    Although this point of view was for some time
central in psychoanalysis, it has been even less
popular in the social sciences than theories of
biological defect or predisposition. Explicit theories of human nature have simply not been acceptable.
As Travis Hirschi (1969, p. 31) has put it:

> In the good old days, the control theorist could
> simply strip away the 'veneer of civilization'
> and expose man's 'animal impulses' for all to see
> . . . His argument was not that delinquents and
> criminals alone are animals, but that we are all
> animals, and thus are naturally capable of com-
> mitting criminal acts.

Since our *awakening* to the dominance of man's environment over his animal nature, such talk has rarely been
heard. Even psychoanalysts are nowadays reluctant to
locate man's deviance in his runaway animal instincts.
Even Freud's emphasis on biological motivation, and
the id, was gradually eroded away by neo-Freudian
views, and the reliance of modern psychiatry on social
science theory emphasizing environmental causes of
deviance is virtually complete.

Today, a few social scientists are beginning to
return to man's nature as an explanation for his deviance. David Matza, for example, assumes that it is as
much a part of man's nature to deviate as to conform.
Others would agree, but most would also probably share
A. K. Cohen's concern for the adequacy of explaining
deviance in terms of man's animal nature. Cohen
points out that most people who commit deviant acts do
so only occasionally: "For example, most students who
cheat and even most children who steal do so only on
occasion and behave 'normally' most of the time. To
explain why *this* person commits this deviant act at
this time, it is therefore necessary to go beyond the
purview of control theory and require borrowings
from other types of theory" (1966, p. 62). Cohen
might have added that if it is human nature to deviate then we must also ask why some people deviate
more than others.

However much human nature may be deficient as
an explanation of deviance, if we review these five
major explanatory positions we will discover that
each depends upon an *assumption* about human nature.
Social strain and sub-cultural theories assume that
man is naturally a conformist; these theories

therefore look to society or culture to explain his
deviance. Psychological theories, for the most part,
make the same assumption but look to individual learning experiences for an explanation of deviance.
Theories of aberrant biology assume the same thing,
finding deviance to reside only in men whose normal,
and hence conformist, biology is defective. Only the
last theory—man as a natural deviant—wholeheartedly
assumes the opposite, locating the sources of deviance
as well as sources of conformity in human nature, just
as they are also to be found in the social and cultural environment.

These five explanations can be, and often have
been, used in various combinations, but for our purpose
of comparing existing explanatory points of view it is
useful to separate them. Keep in mind also that these
explanations are, for better or worse, "scientific"
ones which we as sociologists, psychologists, or anthropologists use to understand what *we* call deviant
phenomena. The improvement of such explanations is
a primary goal of any science, of course, but science
may also profit by examining phenomena in its own
terms—in this case by examining trouble-engendering
rule violations as these are construed and acted upon
by the participants themselves.

ACCOUNTS: INSIDERS' EXPLANATIONS

We have been speaking of deviance as rule violation
that evokes the criticism, anger, outrage, or punitive action of others. This sort of definition is
widely used by social scientists, but even at this
basic level of definition there are disagreements,
some of which are hotly contested (McHugh, 1970;
Schur, 1971). For example, whose rule is being
violated? Should we refer to *deviance* when it is a
private rule held by only one person? Or must the
rule be widely shared and hence be seen by most people
as *legitimate*? Can we properly speak of *deviance*
unless the person who violates a rule intended to do
so? Must *deviant* rule violation discredit the

violator? Should *deviance* be reserved to refer only
to persons who are set aside as different from others
because of their rule violations? All these issues
are scientifically relevant but they refer to *our*
concept—*deviance*. The people whose troublesome rule
violations we choose to refer to as deviance may use a
different term or none at all. In seeking their own
perspective on rule violators, we study their words,
their actions, their explanations. We do so to be
certain that what we study is set in its appropriate
situational context, because knowledge of the situation itself is essential to an understanding and explanation of troublesome rule violation wherever it
occurs.

First, it is important to note that behavior can
often vary greatly without any rule being violated or
any punitive action becoming necessary. For example,
we tolerate great variation in dress without comment,
although we do regard some kinds of dress as insult-
ing, improper or even indecent. All societies provide
for acceptable variation in many areas of behavior.
We know when these limits of acceptable variation
have been exceeded because there is "trouble" in the
form of complaint, accusation, retaliation, and the
like. Trouble, whether it sets an entire community
against one man or merely brings two individuals into
conflict, calls our attention to the rule violation
itself, to its antecedents and its consequences. Its
consequences are usually a central concern. It may
be useful to think of this as a process that begins
when a person commits an act that leads to trouble.
Before this trouble can be resolved, the interested
parties usually call for an *account* (i.e., an explanation, verbal or non-verbal, concerning why the act
occurred) in order that they may determine which consequences should follow. For example, a student
enters class fifteen minutes late for the twelfth
time in that one semester. The professor asks him to
remain after class and provide an explanation (account)
of his behavior. Since he is obviously displeased,
he anticipates the possibility of unpleasant

consequences. Instead of telling the professor the
"truth"—that he prefers to talk to his girlfriend
whom he can only see at that hour of the day—he con-
siders making up a story that might satisfy the professor. His behavior will depend on how he sees
himself (as the soul of honesty, for example), how
he sees his professor (as a person without humor or
understanding), how much he cares about a grade,
and on many other considerations.

Let us look for a moment at each step in this
process. First, we have the person who commits the
troublesome act. People everywhere live in a world
of meaning that includes goals and intentions, or
motives if you prefer. All people are both con-
sciously or unconsciously limited in what they attempt to do by their biology, their beliefs, their
understanding of the situation, their conception of
themselves and others, their personality and a host
of similar factors. Therefore, as a person lives
through any day, he must be aware of his society's
rules—that is, the expectations that other people
have regarding appropriate behavior—his expectations
about the behavior of others, and a generalized set
of understandings about what is right, proper, al-
lowable, etc.

Not all people see all rules in the same way, however. Even in the simplest of societies, not everyone understands all the rules, and some people, for
example, children or the senile, may "know" relatively
little. Many rules, in fact, are not completely clear
to begin with and their legitimacy is not always fully
agreed upon by all. Moreover, almost every rule is
contingent upon a person's status, what the situation
might be, and the intentions of the people involved.
Thus, Watergate to the contrary notwithstanding, it
remains the case that presidents, kings, and people
of great wealth are seldom called into account in the
same way as persons of more limited prestige or power.
There are also situations, statuses, and conditions
that allow or even require reduced responsibility for
persons who engage in certain kinds of behavior that

would ordinarily be deviant. Such occasions or conditions are akin to calling "time out" (MacAndrew and Edgerton, 1969). In our own society, for example, we have occasions such as Mardi Gras or the annual Christmas party where certain behaviors (sexual joking, flirting, drunkenness, etc.) that might otherwise be considered troublesome are not only overlooked but even expected. Similarly, there are social statuses or roles that reduce responsibility for certain kinds of behavior. For example, neither an alcoholic, a psychotic, nor a blind person is held to account for his behavior in the same way that most people are. Moreover, there are many temporary conditions which offer exemptions to people who can successfully demonstrate their entitlement to them, such as extreme grief, fatigue, illness, and psychological stress.

It is little wonder then, that people sometimes act in ways that offend others, and when people are offended, this can mean trouble in such forms as dispute, conflict, revenge, or formal sanction, to mention but a few. People are usually aware that rule violation can have unpleasant consequences. Before turning to these consequences, we should note that the person who violates a rule can become a *trouble-maker* by his own accusation as well as by the accusation of others. Thus people sometimes blame and punish themselves for what they see as their own wrongdoing. They call themselves into account. The result may be shame, guilt, despair, even suicide, or it may be a determination to improve. More often, however, it would appear that others do the accusing, and this accusation often calls for an account—an explanation of the troublesome rule violation. The study of such accounts has produced a small literature of high quality, beginning perhaps with Max Weber and Kenneth Burke, achieving prominence in the work of C. Wright Mills (1940), and being advanced by British scholars such as Austin (1961), Hart (1960), and Peters (1958). A thorough review has been provided by Scott and Lyman (1968), with a contrary position available in Blum and McHugh (1971).

In general, accounts can be seen as *exacerbating* the trouble, *excusing* it, or *justifying* it. Each can take various forms. There are also tactics for avoiding accounts altogether or for apologizing without providing any specific account at all. As Goffman (1971) has observed, some exchanges of this kind are intended to remedy the existing trouble, but others appear to be largely ritualistic and have little to do with the trouble at hand. In some societies, including our own, there may be no request for an account at all. For example, Gluckman (Moore, 1972, p. 63) refers to instances in Africa in which no account for wrongdoing is requested because the wrongdoer's intent is irrelevant. In these cases, liability for rule violation is strictly interpreted and no one cares to hear an excuse or a justification. The application of strict liability of this sort does not appear to be widespread in the world's societies, however. In our own society, many forms of trouble that occur publicly are simply ignored, even by the person most offended or injured, apparently because a confrontation with a stranger is more time-consuming, embarrassing, or dangerous than it is worth.

An important point to remember is that accounts are asked for and are given with an eye toward the consequences of the trouble that is at issue. What should be done? Accounts explain the troublemaker's intent or his motives—his anger, forgetfulness, heroism, provocation, fatigue, fear, confusion, compulsion, insanity, negligence, etc. Accounts serve to explain why the act occurred as it did and what should be done about it. For example, if a plea for justification is successful, the presumed troublemaker may be rewarded or praised. If not, various sanctions may be imposed. These may include labeling the troublemaker as a certain kind of person (e.g., thief, coward, witch) who is thereby discredited as dangerous, disgusting, or the like. Because the stakes are often high, accounts can be serious matters. The outcome is rarely predetermined, however, and the process is usually more akin to a negotiation than to a mechanical or impartial effort to support propriety or to administer justice.

In some of the examples of *trouble* that follow, we shall catch glimpses of all of these aspects of the process whereby people get into and out of trouble. Seeing these matters as the participants do is not only important in its own right, but it will greatly facilitate our efforts to explain such troublesome behavior in scientific terms.

Chapter 3

"Deviance" in Cross-Cultural Perspective

This section illustrates eight categories of trouble-some behavior with examples taken from so-called "folk" societies. All eight categories are frequently re-garded as serious forms of "deviance" in the West, and all commonly occur and are troublesome in the world's folk societies. These categories are useful in illus-trating various points about deviance; they do not necessarily represent the most common or serious forms of deviance in any particular folk society. The various examples are presented for several reasons. First, they illustrate how different cultures view various behaviors that are seen as being troublesome. They also illustrate ways in which the five "scientific" explanations of deviance can be applied, and they some-times reveal the insiders' explanations as well. In addition, these examples provide some basis for an evaluation of the folk-urban distinction and the theories which rest upon it.

Before turning to the examples, it is important to say something further about the concept, "folk," and the process by which these examples from "folk" societies were chosen. In anthropology today, the term "folk" is seldom used. Other general societal terms such as "pre-literate" or "non-Western," and more specific terms such as "hunting and gathering," "stratified," or "peasant," are more often employed

32

as ways of characterizing types of societies. There
are many reasons for this that do not concern us here,
but one point is important. Redfield defines "folk"
as an ideal society as opposed to urban society, and
he provides criteria by which a society's "folkness"
can be identified (small, isolated, homogeneous, non-
literate, etc.). However, since for Redfield "folk"
is an ideal type, no actual society could match it
perfectly; real societies could only approximate it.
Hence, the term folk has inherent limitations either
as a generic or specific term for actual societies.
In addition, Redfield sometimes excludes certain
societies from his folk type *not* because the societies fail to meet his criteria for folkness, but
because members of these societies fail to *behave*
as he believed they should. Thus, for example, the
Siriono, a hunting and gathering society in the tropical forest of Bolivia, were unquestionably small,
isolated, homogeneous, non-literate and aware of their
group solidarity, at least vis-a-vis outsiders. That
is, they clearly met every one of Redfield's explicit
criteria for a folk society. In behavior, however,
the Siriono were not folklike, being highly individualistic and often downright deviant, as we shall see
in a moment. As a result, Redfield excluded the Siriono from his folk type (Redfield, 1955, p. 145).
     Unlike Redfield, we shall include examples from
the Siriono because they meet all of Redfield's criteria for such societies. We refer to them as "folk"
in order to keep the important theoretical distinctions
of the folk-urban theory clearly in mind. There are
several systems available today for ranking the
relative simplicity or complexity of societies (see
Naroll and Cohen, 1971). In addition to meeting Redfield's general criteria, the examples presented here
are from societies that these ranking systems agree
belong well down the scale toward simplicity.
     Specific examples from these societies were
chosen to illustrate issues raised earlier about
deviant behavior. Neither the societies themselves,
nor the examples from them, were selected by any

sampling procedure. Indeed, the present limited
knowledge about *deviant* behavior in *folk* societies
precludes the use of any such systematic procedure.
We can only rarely say how much deviance occurs in
any given society or in any type of society. This
is so because we must rely upon what anthropologists
have written about deviance and only rarely have anthropologists made a systematic, quantitative study
of deviance in a folk society.

THEFT AND REFUSAL TO SHARE

Theft (which may not be universal but *is* extremely
common) and refusal to share or cooperate (which
very well may be universal) often produce trouble.
In either case one person places his or her personal
interests above the legitimate interests of another
person or group. Many anthropologists have noted
that theft is rare in very simple societies, perhaps
because personal property is minimal, personally
earmarked, or available to anyone for the asking.
An intriguing example comes from the Trobriand
Islands of Melanesia where it was reported (Bronislaw
Malinowski, 1926, pp. 117-118) that theft was "humili-
ating" and hence was only done by "feebleminded,
social outcasts, or minors." The reference here to
social outcasts is intriguing. Did they become labeled as outcasts because they stole, or did they
steal because they were outcasts and hence excused?
We are not told. Another interesting early report
comes from an equally famous source, A. R. Radcliffe-
Brown, who reported that theft was especially repug-
nant to the Andamanese (who live on small islands off
the coast of Burma) because any material object might
be had merely for the asking, requiring only a recip-
rocal gift at a later time (1922, p. 41). Nevertheless, and to Radcliffe-Brown's surprise, theft *did*
occur among the Andamanese and when it did, it let
loose a set of consequences that included vitupera-
tion, displays of temper, and spear throwing. In

short, it made trouble. But this should really not be
surprising, for in fact most small societies have
thieves, some of whom become labeled as such (Bowen,
1964).

In other folk societies, people may cause trouble
by refusing to share. For example, Elizabeth Thomas
has provided us with a sensitive and detailed descrip-
tion of life among the Kung Bushmen of the Kalahari
Desert. These hunters and gatherers depend upon harmony and cooperation for their very survival and yet
some Bushmen refuse to share food even though their
rules call for them to do so. It is also apparent
that children are slow to accept the necessity of
sharing (1958, p. 117).

Let us look at a folk society somewhat more
closely. The Siriono live in small hunting and gathering bands in the tropical forest of Eastern Bolivia
(Holmberg, 1969). Their environment is difficult, at
best, and despite their occasional horticultural efforts they are frequently on the edge of starvation,
as was anthropologist A. R. Holmberg who stayed with
them during their famine. Holmberg comments repeatedly on the troublemaking propensities of the Siriono.
He says, for example, ". . . although one of the important legal norms is that of sharing food within the
extended family, such sharing rarely occurs unless the
supply of food is abundant" (1969, p. 150). We need
hardly add that sharing is most important when food is
not abundant. "Indeed, sharing rarely occurs without
a certain amount of mutual distrust and misunderstand-
ing; a person always feels that it is he who is being
taken advantage of" (Holmberg, 1969, p. 151). So
pervasive is this fear that many simply will not share
as their culture calls for them to do. Instead, when
their few crops ripen, men refuse to go hunting on
the grounds that their women will eat the maize crop
while they are gone. Men also suspect women of
hoarding meat. Holmberg quotes one Siriono man as
follows: "When someone comes near the house, women
hide the meat; they cover it with leaves. When you
ask them where the meat is they tell you there is

none. They eat it in the night and steal off to the
forest to eat. Women even push meat up their vaginas
to hide it" (1969, p. 155). Holmberg provides many
other comparable examples indicating that many, even
most, Siriono do not follow their own rules about
sharing food.

It is tempting to think of the Siriono as an
anomaly, a people torn apart by their hunger, but the
Siriono are not unique in their selfish refusal to do
what they themselves agree is right. The Ik of Uganda,
for example, are far worse (Turnbull, 1972). The Ik,
who were in fact starving when Turnbull saw them, not
only refused to share food, but they literally snatched
food out of the mouths of those too weak to repel them,
even if those people were their fathers, brothers,
wives, or children. Eskimos provide another example
of refusal to share; they are expected to lend their
wives to friends with good will. In fact, however, the
practice seldom reflects good will. Instead it commonly leads to sexual jealousy and violence. Rasmussen (1927, p. 250) found that in one community of Musk
Ox Eskimo in Canada, all the adult males in the fifteen
separate families that made up this community in the
1920's had been involved either as a principal or
accessory in a homicide involving a quarrel over a
woman.

Such brief treatments of complex phenomena may be
more tantalizing than fulfilling. Therefore, I recom-
mend a careful reading of Colin Turnbull's books on
the Mbuti Pygmies of the Ituri Forest, *The Forest People* (1961) and *The Wayward Servants* (1965). These two
books provide a rich report of a people whose hunting
livelihood in their forest environment requires cooperation and harmony, yet who somehow fall short of full
compliance with their most central rules. Turnbull
tells us one thing that the Pygmies abhor, and "never"
do, is steal from one another. Nearby Bantu-speaking
villagers steal, but they are only "animals" and so
the Pygmies happily steal from them. But Pygmies
simply do not steal from each other. It would shatter
their harmony and it would disrupt the cooperation

required for a successful hunt. Faced with the realities of Pygmy life, however, Turnbull hedges: "This
is not to say that theft of food never takes place.
It would be a rare Mbuti woman who did not conceal a
portion of the catch in case she was forced to share
with others . . . ." (1965, p. 198). What is more,
this is not the only type of theft that Turnbull
reports. For example, on one occasion two spears
and a basket of meat were stolen from a woman. Rather
than pursue an investigation of so reprehensible an
offense, the Pygmies ignored it (1965, p. 214). Finding and dealing with such a thief was apparently too
serious for the Pygmies to consider. Mbuti society
was also represented by at least one labeled thief.
This man, Pepei, was a bachelor with no woman to cook
for him so he stole food. Like any other Pygmy, Pepei
should not steal, but he was a wonderfully comic story-
teller and he often stole from people who were temporarily unpopular, so he was usually tolerated. On
occasions, however, he stole too much, or from the
wrong person, and then he was whipped and forced to
spend the night alone in the forest. In a small band
of Pygmies who do not permit theft, it is odd indeed
to find Pepei, a known thief, and at least one other
unknown thief as well.

It is odder still to find Cephu. Cephu was
neither a very good nor very popular hunter, but he
was a Mbuti. Thus, it came as a shock to Turnbull
and to the Pygmies themselves when he committed "one
of the most heinous crimes in Pygmy eyes" (1961, p.
109) by secretly setting up his hunting net in front
of the others in an effort to capture the first wave
of animals that were being driven toward it. Unfortunately for Cephu, he was discovered. It is our
good fortune that Turnbull recorded the ensuing
account in some detail, for this episode now provides a fine example of deviance as it is discovered,
discussed, punished, and finally, smoothed over
(1961, pp. 94-110). Most clearly of all, we see how
the Pygmies—perhaps like many of us—are more concerned
with repairing important personal relationships than

they are with administering justice. From it we
learn much about how the Pygmies saw this "crime" and
how they related it to Cephu's past and present circumstances. It is a classic account.

Do we have a satisfactory explanation for Cephu,
or Pepei, or the murderous Eskimos, or the stingy
Siriono? We do not, not with any confidence at least.
The reasons for this may become clearer after we
discuss more examples of deviance and then return to
an appraisal of the adequacy of our explanations for
such acts.

In attempting to explain deviant theft or the
refusal to share, one always asks for more information, even for a case as well-documented as that of
Cephu. This is a good lesson, for it illustrates the
complexity of any single deviant act and cautions us
not to attempt simplistic explanations. Some scientists would quickly acknowledge this, but would argue
that no single case of human behavior can be "explained" in scientific terms; one must have many
cases in order to find patterns and discover explanations. The soundness of this position depends upon
what one means by "explanation," and this is an issue
that we shall discuss later, but it is well to remember
that even when patterns can be detected, they are
made up of complex individual cases like that of
Cephu.

The widespread occurrence of deviant theft and
non-sharing raises another question. If these acts
of deviance are common in human societies, do the
causes lie, as Hobbes would have said, in human
nature? And if it is human nature to steal or to be
selfish, then why does only a minority do so? Or is
it always only a minority? Turnbull reports that the
Ik of Uganda are so close to starvation that no one
shares food, and everyone steals food if they can
(1972). But even among the Ik, things were not always
so bad and evidence of social strain is obvious. In
other societies, it is possible that deviant theft
and non-sharing are related to psychological defense
or commitment, or even to defective biology. And if,

as among the Siriono, it is women who most often refuse to share, we might even speculate that a female
sub-culture is involved.

   This first category of deviance, then, calls into
possible use the full list of explanations of deviant
behavior without clearly indicating which one provides
the best understanding for any given society or for
all of them. It is clear that folk societies, like
urban societies, have thieves and selfish persons. We
do not know why.

SUICIDE

Suicide in the West is typically thought to be as
tragic as it is troublesome. We have civil laws and
religious proscriptions against it. If a suicide attempt fails, the result can be a deviant identity; if
it succeeds, the survivors must often live with a
"taint." For example, until 1961 any survivor of a
suicide attempt was subject to criminal penalty, and,
as Hamlet made clear, a person who succeeded in killing himself was liable to be punished by being denied
a Christian burial. Nevertheless, it is generally
estimated that on the order of 10 to 12 persons per
100,000 commit suicide in England and the United
States each year. The frequency of suicide is seldom
measured with great accuracy, but in the West the rate
of suicide is thought to vary with such socially relevant factors as high social status, age, sex, religion, marital status, ethnicity, occupation, and edu-
cation, to mention but a few. In some countries,
these rates vary dramatically, as, for example, in
Egypt, where the general Moslem suicide rate is 2 per
100,000, but 21.5 for the divorced and 36.6 for the
well-educated (Khalil, 1962). Countries also vary
from one to another, with Chile reporting 4.4 per
100,000, Japan 20.5, and Austria close to 40. Catho-
lic countries generally have low rates, perhaps because the act is so deviant that it occurs less,
perhaps because the strong religious condemnation of

suicide leads people to conceal its occurrence. Suicide, then, is profoundly influenced by social and
cultural considerations (DeVos, 1968).

     In some societies, suicide is not deviant at all.
On the contrary, it is positively valued. We are all
familiar with the Japanese attitude toward hara-kiri,
or seppuku, a form of ritual disembowlment which was
the proper course of action for disgraced noblemen
or defeated military leaders. The use of young men
as Kamikaze pilots in World War II is another familiar
example of suicide as a culturally valued act, at
least in time of war. Similarly, the wife of a Brah-
man who threw herself on his funeral pyre in "suttee"
would be highly praised, and among a number of North
American Indian tribes, it was an approved act for a
warrior to commit suicide by facing his enemies without weapons or by tying himself to the ground so
that he could not possibly escape the lances or
arrows of his enemies.

     In other societies, suicide may be seen as un-
fortunate but necessary. Thus, in Highland New
Guinea a Bena Bena woman whose husband has just died
may decide to kill herself rather than be inherited
by another man. If this is her decision, she will
call upon her brother for assistance. He bends
over under a tree limb and she stands on his back
while affixing the noose. At her signal he walks
away. He may be very fond of his sister, but he
sees the decision as hers to make without interfer-
ence. Such suicide may disturb the man who would
otherwise have inherited the widow, but no rule is
violated, and no trouble results (Langness, 1972).
Similarly, the Eskimos sometimes resorted to suicide
in order to survive in their harsh environments.
Therefore, an old or sick person who could no longer
make an economic contribution had the right to demand
that a kinsman assist him in suicide. This was rarely a happy task but it was an obligation, and it was
carried out dutifully whether the person was to be
strangled, pushed off the ice, over a cliff, or simply
abandoned. Weyer records the example of an old Eskimo

man who felt that he could no longer contribute what
he thought he should as a member of the group. The
old man asked his son, who was about twelve years old,
to sharpen a big hunting knife. "Then he indicated
the vulnerable spot over his heart where his son
should stab him. The boy plunged the knife deep, but
the stroke failed to take effect. The old father
suggested with dignity and resignation, "'Try it a
little higher my son'" (1924, p. 138). The second try
succeeded. There was no deviance in this suicide;
rather, there was a poignant effort to follow a sadly
necessary rule. Deviance here would have involved a
refusal by the old man to choose death or refusal by
his son to carry out the request.

Other societies view suicide with only mild re-
gret. The Tikopia of the Solomon Islands seem to
regard suicide as a natural, if somewhat regrettable,
act as long as the motive and method are reasonable
(Firth, 1961). Thus, among these people there is a
high suicide rate by hanging, swimming out to sea, or
putting off to sea in a canoe, for which acceptable
motives include grief, marital discord, and severe
illness. In some cases, such suicides may be thought
quite commendable. But some suicides are not fully
accepted, as when the person's method is bizarre, or
his motives unreasonable. These acts cause trouble
and those who attempt suicide, should they survive,
could well become deviant persons. Firth records the
following case admitting that the Tikopia sometimes
use "odd" ways to commit suicide:

> About the oddest was that chosen by Pu Sao, who
> having broken wind in a public gathering, in his
> shame climbed a coconut palm and sat down on the
> sharp-pointed, hard flower spathe, which pierced
> his fundament and killed him—a bizarre case of
> making the punishment fit the crime. (1961, p. 4)

Some societies dread suicide. The Mohave Indians,
who are so concerned with suicide that they believe
even infants can intentionally kill themselves, regard
the act as highly deviant (Devereux, 1961). Suicide

is extremely troublesome in many other societies as
well. Malinowski's famous account of a Trobriand
suicide is a case in point. A boy of 16 had been
maintaining an incestuous relationship with his maternal cousin. The relationship was known to many
but when the girl's ex-lover complained and insulted
the boy publicly, his shame drove him to suicide. He
climbed a palm tree and addressed the community which
had assembled below him. His words were not penitent,
however, they were an explanation of his love for the
girl and a threat against the young man who accused
him. He then jumped to his death, but his words compelled his clansmen to exact revenge upon the man
who had accused him, and this they did on at least
two violent occasions known to Malinowski (1926).

Linking revenge to suicide can be very troublesome indeed, and it occurs in many parts of the world.
Fortune (1932) notes that a Dobuan man whose wife was
flagrantly unfaithful might commit suicide in order to
induce his lineage to avenge his death upon his wife.
A similar pattern is widespread in tribal Africa
(Bohannan, 1960). In many African societies it is
not uncommon for a young woman to love a young man,
only to find that her father and brothers insist that
she marry an older and wealthier man who can afford
an ample bride-price. Should the girl refuse, or try
to run away, she may be coerced, even beaten, until
she agrees to the marriage. Some young women prefer
hanging to such a marriage. The consequences for the
over-zealous father and brothers can be quite serious.
Such a suicide is an economic blow, not only to the
father and brothers, but to the clan at large. There
will be no bride-price for her—ever—and the reputation
of the family and the clan suffer. In some instances,
angered clansmen may impose a fine upon the father.
The father, then, has lost his bride-price, been
fined, and must thereafter contend with a bereaved
mother and sundry other relatives. Faced with such
trouble, it is little wonder that a daughter's threat
to kill herself is a powerful one, and the act itself
is seen, particularly by men, as highly deviant. In

other instances, a wife may kill herself in order to call attention to her husband's mistreatment of her.

Obviously, then, suicide can be a serious form of deviance. It is somewhat unique because the trouble it brings primarily affects the living, and it is they who accuse and defend, and who label—the dead as well as the living.

Suicide is notable for the variation of its form, frequency, and motivation from culture to culture. In some folk societies it occurs rarely, perhaps never. In others, it occurs but is not considered to be deviant. In still others, it is a heinous offense. Suicide also offers limitless examples for each of the major explanations of deviance discussed earlier. Durkheim's classic research made a strong case for social strain and anomie as causes of suicide (1897). Many other sociologists have reported sub-cultural considerations in suicide (Wiele, 1960), and psychological explanations are so numerous as to defy summary (Hippler, 1969). Biological factors related to injury, sickness, and aging are also obvious. And more than one psychoanalyst since Freud has explained suicide through man's natural wish for death. We might do well to note at this point that suicide, like many categories of deviance, is a category, nothing more. Thus, from culture to culture, it takes many forms, and probably can be comprehended in one society or another by all of the "explanations" listed in Chapter One.

VIOLENCE

Violence (physical force used with the intent to injure) is an obvious source of trouble in folk societies. Yet it is probably correct to say that violence is not universal, and even when it does occur it is by no means always troublesome. Thus, there are societies such as the people of Ifaluk Atoll in Micronesia (Burrows & Spiro, 1953) where adult violence does not occur at all, and others such as the Mixtec Indians of Mexico (Romney & Romney, 1963) where adult violence is so rare that only one instance was seen

during a year of study, and according to the Mixtec,
that was possible only by virtue of the violent man's
indulgence in alcohol and marijuana together.   In
other folk societies, violence is confined to special
occasions, special persons, or is always sub-lethal.
In still others, such as the Bushmen or the Siriono,
serious violence is uncommon, but occurs now and then
with serious trouble as the consequence (Thomas, 1958;
Holmberg, 1969).

On the other hand, some folk societies are immensely violent.   South American Indian societies
alone provide a full range of violence.   The Kaingang
of Brazil (Henry, 1941) were engaged in such a continuous cycle of blood vengeance between extended
families that when Henry met them they had been reduced to but a remnant of their former population.
Yet the Kaingang did not permit murder within the
extended family and over their 200 years of remembered
history, this rule was known to have been violated
only once.   The Yamana of Tierra del Fuego (Gusinde,
1961) were so unremittingly hostile to one another
that they were engaged in a seemingly endless round
of brawls and murders between families despite the
fact that such violence was clearly proscribed.   The
Yanomamo Indians of Brazil and Ecuador are exceedingly
warlike.   They are also violent within their own villages, engaging in formalized contests of painful
chest-pounding, side-slapping, and head-bashing which
sometimes erupt into general mayhem.   All of this
violence is culturally appropriate, but deviant violence occurs as well (Chagnon, 1968).

There are some excellent descriptions of violent
deviance now available.   For example, Peter Matthies-
sen (1962) has provided such an account of the Kurelu
in the western highlands of New Guinea.   The Kurelu
are a warlike people who prize martial courage and
manly strength.   The "big man" who is aggressive and
domineering is their ideal.   Not surprisingly, there
are Kurelu men who lack the requisite courage,
strength, and aggressivity to be a "big man" and some
of these men become deviants because they are not

violent enough. But, it is also possible for Kurelu
men to break rules by being excessively violent, and
such men, too, can be troublesome and become deviants.
    June Nash (1967) has provided a detailed analysis
of homicide in the Maya Indian township of Teklum in
Mexico. In recent years, due to changes in the social
organization and economy, homicide has increased
sharply, and Nash gives details of 37 murders occur-
ring from 1938 to 1965. This is a murder rate of
more than 250 per 100,000, compared to 32 per 100,000
for Mexico as a whole and 4.8 per 100,000 for the United States. In Teklum, homicide is a male activity;
all the victims and the killers were men. Many men
were killed because they were suspected of witchcraft,
and these killings were generally seen by the resi-
dents of Teklum as justified (the Mexican police were
helpless to intervene without community support).
Other killings, however, were not justifiable. In
the case of these killings, accounts were requested
and serious consequences followed. Nash's analysis
yields a particularly rich variety of material
describing violent deviance through the eyes of the
participants themselves.
    It is possible to read reports of individuals
in folk societies whose violence, or their aversion to
it, has made them deviant. My account of a man from
the Pokot people of Northwest Kenya illustrates the
point that even in a violent society (the Pokot are a
cattle-herding people who esteem bravery and military
success) it is possible to be far too violent (Edgerton, 1969). A man, Amalung, had achieved prominence
among the Pokot by virtue of his intimidating physical presence and aggressiveness. He was a powerful
and menacing man. Other Pokot feared but admired
Amalung. Amalung was jealous of his brother whose
cattle he coveted. He often accused this brother of
being a dangerous madman who should be done away with
for the good of all. This brother was generally
known to drink a bit much but no one thought that he
was mad or dangerous. Without public cooperation,

Amalung had to take matters into his own hands, literally. With the help of another man, he killed his own
brother by, among other things, tearing his testicles
off. When this act of violence occurred his public
support vanished, and he was treated as a criminal.
This sort of violence against one's brother was not acceptable. Similarly, Edward Winter (1959) provides
several long autobiographical reports of men whose
violent behavior kept them in continuous trouble among
the Amba people of Uganda. Again the accounts are
most interesting, and most complicated.

Deviance can also take the form of non-violence,
as Regina Flannery's (1960) report of the Gros Ventre
Indian woman, Coming Daylight, demonstrates. In this
Plains Indian society where warfare, fortitude, and
bravery were so prized, some women even became warriors, and most women suffered the loss of a finger-
joint in mourning without protest. Not so in the case
of Coming Daylight. She could not stand the sight of
blood, would not mutilate herself, and detested violence of any sort. She was subjected to ridicule
and coercion, but held her ground throughout her life,
despite being regarded as a deviant.

Violence offers another view of the relativity
of cultural definitions of deviance. A deviant label
may be the penalty for excessive violence in one
society, for the wrong kind of violence in another,
and for too little violence in a third. Again we see
examples of several of the explanations of deviance
discussed earlier. Violence, for example, in Teklum,
has apparently increased due to recent social strain,
but even so there are deviant and non-deviant forms
of homicide. Reports of violence in folk societies
also leave open the possibility of biological and
psychological explanations. Only the human nature
explanation fares badly, since there are non-violent
societies as well as non-violent individuals throughout the world of folk societies, but this issue is
complex and we shall consider it more carefully later
on.

SEXUALITY

Present-day sexual deviance in the urban West is, if
not more common than ever before (remember the Vic-
torians and Krafft-Ebing), then at least a good deal
more visible. Sexual deviance is also quite visible
in most non-Western societies as well; it is almost
certainly universal in occurrence. Needless to say,
like other kinds of deviance, it varies in form and
frequency. The Colombian villagers of Aritama
(Reichel-Dolmatoff & Reichel-Dolmatoff, 1961) complain
about the incidence of incest and bestiality. Shaka
Zulu was not only remarkable for the changes he
brought over a large part of Africa, but for monumental sexual aberrations as well (Fernandez, 1971).
Even the Siriono, who are so lusty a people that one
would almost think that anything goes, have their
sexual deviants. Among the Siriono known to Holmberg was a homosexual man who was thought of as a
woman, not to mention a man named Etoni whose sadis-
tic penchant for wounding the breasts of women during
sexual intercourse had caused him to be shunned by
women altogether (Holmberg, 1969, pp. 196-170).
     Other small societies have their share of sexual
deviants as well. In a small portion of Pokot terri-
tory in Kenya, I was able to locate two intersexed
persons whose external genital anomalies were known
to all. Six others were known in other parts of
Pokotland. The Navaho, like the classical Greeks,
esteemed intersexed persons, but the Pokot thought
them "monsters" who were "worthless." I was told
of several intersexed infants who were killed but
the two persons I met had managed to survive, despite
terrible stigma, largely by virtue of their capacity
for making themselves economically useful (Edgerton,
1964). In a culture like that of the Pokot which so
highly values heterosexual prowess, these sexually
ambiguous persons were profoundly deviant despite
their effort to be normal.
     The Pokot are also notable for another kind of
sexual deviance. They are a people devoted to

beauty and sexual gratification. Both sexes expect
and demand that sexual relations culminate in orgasm
for man and woman alike. Husbands often engage in
adulterous affairs, even though such affairs are dis-
approved of, and they are sometimes unable to satisfy
the sexual demands of their wives (these ladies are
also familiar with adultery but their culpability is
more difficult to determine, at least physiologically).
Should a man fail in his orgasmic duties often enough,
and should this failure be attributed to his adultery
or disinterest, his wife may follow a practice called
kilapat (the shaming party) by assembling her female
friends and tying up the errant husband during his
sleep. These women then subject the husband to
various obscenities of sight, sound, and touch. They
may, for example, defecate upon him; they always
revile him; and they often beat him for good measure.
To make the lesson still more memorable, they finally
slaughter and eat his favorite ox before releasing
him—a battered and humiliated but more dutiful man
when it comes to the conjugal rights of his wife (Edgerton & Conant, 1964).

Among the Pokot, a woman who does not enjoy sex
is called deviant. Only a few hundred miles to the
south in Kenya, the Gusii present a contrasting picture of sexuality and deviance. The Gusii have developed extraordinary sexual antagonism between men and
women. This hostility is expressed in various ways,
not the least of which is a wedding night performance
in which the wife attempts to delay consummation by
any act or artifice (including tying her pubic hair
across her vagina), and the husband takes pride in
his ability to inflict the maximal degree of pain by
his sexual assault (LeVine, 1959). It is not surprising to learn that Gusii women who enjoy sex are seen
as deviant, and that Gusii men have achieved an excep-
tionally high frequency of rape (in 1955-56 the figure
was 47.2 per 100,000 compared to 13.9 for the urban
United States).

Perhaps we should never be surprised by the
wondrous variety that cultures provide in regard to

sexual deviance. Consider, for example, E. E. Evans-
Pritchard's report of institutionalized homosexuality
among the Azande of the Sudan.   Like many East African
societies, the Azande sent their young men to live together in bachelor barracks while they performed years
of military service. These warriors were forbidden
to marry during their military years, and since all
available girls were engaged while very young, they
had to find sexual satisfaction with younger boys.
Warriors not only regularly established homosexual
relationships with younger boys (ages 12-20) but actually married them in a temporary union.   Bride-price
was paid, the boys performed female tasks, and the
couple slept together, having intra-crural intercourse.
All this was entirely approved. What is more, these
homosexual years had no permanent effect on sex-role
performance.   Both warrior husbands and boy-wives
eventually married women and had a normal married life.
Women among the Azande, however, were not granted comparable privileges. Wives in polygynous households
which were typically headed by an aging man, were often
sexually neglected and some of these women established
homosexual relationships.   These women carved a phallus
from a sweet potato or manioc root, and they alternated
in the male and female role.   Yet men looked upon such
relationships with revulsion, and women who were appre-
hended in lesbianism could be put to death (Evans-Pritchard, 1970).   Here we have a particularly striking
example of how social strain can lead to homosexuality
by males and females alike.   In one case, however,
homosexual behavior was defined as appropriate while
in the other case, it was punishable by death.
     Sexual deviance may also be undertaken in the
face of great disapproval yet bring about far-reaching
social changes. The literature is filled with cases
of young people who have indulged in incestuous relationships as long as they were "discreet," but when
discretion slipped away accounts were demanded. The
consequences, as among the Mbuti Pygmies, were usually
mild. Leo Pospisil has provided an instance in which
incest led to far more dramatic consequences. Pospisil

reports the incestuous activities of Awaiitigaaj, a
Kapauku New Guinean, who was the headman of a village,
a prosperous owner of pigs, a brave leader in war,
and more than something of a lecher. Like any true
connoisseur of female beauty, he pursued his interests devotedly, marrying ten of the most attractive
women in the area. Unfortunately, he discovered
that the incest taboo—which prohibited marriage between individuals of the same sib—would deprive him
of an "outstanding example of female pulchritude"
(1958, p. 832). To shorten the story, the headman
married her nonetheless, then fled to avoid the traditional penalty for incest which was execution. After
some complicated maneuvering between the relatives on
both sides, the girl's relatives made a tactical error
in the negotiations and were compelled to accept the
incestuous union. Pospisil concludes that out of
this act of sexual deviance a precedent was established which destroyed the existing incest taboo and
eventually brought about an extensive change in the
law and social structure of a larger tribal confeder-
acy. Pospisil continues: "pursuing his own precedent, the headman subsequently married two more
members of his own sib. He also promulgated a new
law, proclaiming that it was now permissible to
marry women of the same village and sib as long as
they were not first paternal parallel cousins"
(p. 833). When Pospisil asked him in public about his
motives, he received the following explanation:

> To marry (a girl of the same sib and generation)
> is good as long as she is a second paternal paral-
> lel cousin. In the old days the people did not
> think of this possibility, but now it is permis-
> sible . . . To marry (such a girl) is not bad, in-
> deed it is nice; in this way one becomes rich.
> (Pospisil, 1958, p. 833)

However, when the headman was questioned in private, he
gave Pospisil this confidential statement:

I think whoever likes any girl should be able to
marry her. I set up the new taboo only in order
to break down the old restrictions. The people
are like that. One has to tell them lies.
(Pospisil, 1958, p. 834)

Elsewhere a person can be labeled as a deviant
for following cultural norms about sexual behavior too
closely. Thus, for example, Henry Selby (1974) tells
us that among the Zapotec Indians of Mexico sexual
activity is supposed to take place exclusively between
husband and wife. He goes on to say that the *only*
person in the community who has followed this rule by
having no extramarital affairs is considered a deviant.
The reasons for these apparently contradictory circumstances are complex. Basically, the person in question—a woman named Guillerma—responded to her husband's
discreet sexual dalliances not by having similar affairs herself, as every other woman did, but by contin-
ually throwing her own virtue in his face, and by
developing disabling headaches. Worse, she informed
the spouses of those who were having illicit sexual
affairs. As a result, she was universally condemned
as an "evil-hearted" person, a category of malicious
deviance which is thought by the Zapotec to be even
worse than witchcraft.

In this section we have seen examples of sexual
deviance, as among the Siriono, that were apparently
attributable to psychological factors. We have seen
other examples, as with the intersexed Pokot, that suggest biological factors. Sexual deviance among the
Azande appears to be related to social and cultural
factors having to do with warfare, polygyny and political dominance by older men. Differences between
the Gusii and Pokot are more difficult to understand,
however, and an explanation of the sexual deviance of
Awaiitigaaj would require more knowledge than we
possess. His public account was skillful, but his
cynical disregard for morality while presenting his
private account makes one wonder. Was he a psychopath? Are there historical reasons why the Pokot

and Gusii took opposite paths? Why was Guillerma so
d..fferent from other Zapotec? Although the answers
are not available, it is useful to ask the questions
here as a means of becoming more sensitive to the
issues that are raised by deviance.

GENERATIONAL CONFLICT

The conflict between generations has been a fashion-
able topic in recent years, but in one form or another
such conflict is universal and the trouble it brings
throws light on another dimension of deviance. In the
United States, so-called *juvenile delinquency* has long
been a major focus of sociological interest in deviance. Recently, the "rebellion" of youth, particularly college students, has heightened this interest
(Mead, 1970). According to many, the young are no
longer expressing their conflict with older generations through violence, irresponsibility, or petu-
lance; they are in *open* rebellion against the values
and institutions of their parents' generation. This
rebellion has not been confined to the West. It has
struck urban Nigeria, for example, with comparable
force. Nigerian periodicals make it quite clear that
the struggle there is seen by youth and their elders
alike as a contest for the power once held so firmly
by the elders (*Drum Magazine*, 1966).
      The conflict of generations in smaller and sim-
pler societies has been recognized by many, from Van
Gennep in 1909 to Eisenstadt in 1956 and Cohen in
1964. For the most part the emphasis has been on the
orderly transition from one age-related status to
another, not upon deviance either as an individual
or collective phenomenon. Others, largely concerned
with socialization, have portrayed relationships
between children and their elders rather like a bat-
tleground, with the older generation doing its best
to tame a new generation of young barbarians. Such
a view yields a picture of the Crow Indians of Montana,
who control their errant youngsters by pouring water

down their noses, or of the Hopi trying to educate
and control their young by initiation ceremonies involving the Kachinas.   In his autobiography, Sun Chief
describes the blows he received from the Kachinas as
whippings for his misbehavior (Simmons, 1942., p. 83):
"I stood them fairly well, without crying, and thought
my suffering was past; but then the Ho Kachina struck
me four more times and cut me to pieces.   I struggled,
yelled, and urinated. . . . Blood was running down
over my body . . . ." The autobiography also reveals
the feelings of young Sun Chief as he came to understand, resent, and rebel against the whipping he
received (Simmons, 1942).

It may or may not be useful to think of generational conflict as deviance.   For example, some geron-
tocratic systems succeed in maintaining the power and
privilege of the old without provoking the young to
overt rebellion.   The Australian aborigines were particularly successful in this regard, being able to
send young men of the Central Desert through a prolonged period of stressful and painful initiations
(extrusion from the band, penile circumcision, urethral
sub-incision, tooth evulsion, etc.) without more than
an occasional individual protest or defection, including the occasional death of an initiate.   This usually
resulted in little trouble for the elders, certainly
not enough to weaken the grip of the old.

For the Samburu of Northern Kenya (Spencer, 1965),
generational conflict was widespread and it threatened
the very continuance of Samburu society.   Like the
Azande to the north, the Samburu relied upon age-
grades of young warriors to protect their borders
against the incursions of cattle-raiding enemies.   The
warriors in the cattle camps were not denied all access
to girls, as were the Azande, but they were forced to
remain bachelors for many years while the elders accu-
mulated wives, often including the girl friends of the
warriors.   While the young men and their young women
were proud of war honors and warrior's prestige, they
also wanted to become elders so that they would have

the right to marry. The resentment of the young increased as they saw the elders accumulating wives and
wealth at their expense. When the elders found more
and more reasons to delay their decision that the most
senior grade of warriors should be allowed to marry,
this resentment boiled over. As a result, warriors
sometimes rebelled with cattle raids that provoked
retaliation, with brawls that threatened social solidarity, and with such disrespect for elders that the
very basis of their power was threatened. When this
disrespect included adultery with the young wives of
the elders, the elders' wrath was especially great.
The elders bullied and wheedled and in desperation
invoked the curse—that magical force they possessed
which was believed capable of bringing illness or
death to its target, the warriors. Both elders and
warriors believed that the other group was wrong and
each was prepared to take serious steps to achieve
what it saw as legitimate goals. The conflict was
serious and endemic, and Spencer reports that the balance of social order among the Samburu was precarious
indeed. The generational trouble of the Samburu is
another useful example of the interplay between social
strain and sub-culture (the culture of the young versus that of the old) leading to behavior that each
sub-culture saw as deviant.
       The countrymen of County Clare, Ireland, provide
an instructive comparison to the Samburu. As described
in the 1930's by anthropologist Conrad Arensberg (1959),
these countrymen granted their old men and women every
bit as much prestige and power as that held by Australian or Samburu elders. The old had great symbolic
prestige, occupying the best room in the house while
their cliques controlled public opinion and political
power. Most important of all, however, was the fact
that they owned the land. All sons had an equal right
to inherit their father's farm, but by the 1930's the
land was so heavily populated that farms could no
longer be subdivided. Instead, each farmer picked one
son to inherit the farm, then arranged for that son's

marriage. Like the Samburu, Irish countrymen found
reasons why the transfer of their farm to a chosen
son should be delayed. So great was the delay likely
to be that, throughout Ireland, 62% of all males were
unmarried between the ages of thirty and thiry-five
(42% of women in the same age group were unmarried)
and 25% of all males were unmarried by the time they
reached fifty (the same was true of women). Marriage
was even later in some parts of the country. Until a
man was married he was still a "boy," literally,
although he might be over 50 years of age. He was
called a boy, had few privileges, and fewer rights.
Many sons, having little hope of inheriting their
father's farm, emigrated, while others went to towns
or cities or to the Church. Some stayed in the countryside and expressed rebellious thoughts about the
old and their power (Arensberg, 1959, pp. 59, 165-166).
While this system continued to maintain itself at the
time Arensberg studied it, social order was clearly
dependent upon the outmigration of most of the young,
the patience of the few sons who were chosen to inherit land, and the women who were destined to marry
such men. While the system perpetuates itself, it
also creates great resentment, as has been so poi-
gnantly documented by generations of Irish novelists.
     The conflict of generations can also be seen in
the privilege sometimes accorded to senior men or
women in Kenya. An evocative illustration comes from
an account of Kisese, an elderly Kamba man in Kenya
(Lindblom, 1920). One evening after imbibing far too
much beer he staggered into a nearby house to sleep
it off. By ill chance, he chose his mother-in-law's
house and the Kamba maintain an extreme avoidance
relationship between a man and his mother-in-law.
When Kisese awoke in the morning he became aware of
this profound breach of decorum. So did everyone
else in the vicinity. Kisese was no ordinary man,
however. He was an elder who had been a war leader,
and he was wealthy. So he sent to his home for a fat
ox and some goats which he presented to his mother-
in-law, declaring that from that time on the

avoidance between them was at an end. A younger or less important man could never have managed such a tour de force. As Lindblom (1920, p. 91) put it, "If he had been a youth, it would probably have cost him dear, but as he was a rich and influential man, he got his way." For young Kamba who were forced literally to dive off paths into thorn bushes to avoid their mothers-in-law when they met them, the inequality was said to have been galling. We often think of juvenile delinquency but it is worthwhile to think, as young Kamba might, of senior (or senile) delinquency as well.

Trouble between generations can be a serious form of deviance, especially when the generations become named (or otherwise given distinction) and have differing rights and privileges. Unlike the other forms of deviance we have considered, this one is often collective and its causes seem to lie primarily in social strain and sub-cultural conflict.

PSYCHOACTIVE DRUGS

Concern with alcohol and various psychoactive drugs or "narcotics" in the social sciences has progressed from an early moralism, through a strong interest in labeling, to a recent flurry of politically charged pronouncements. Cross-cultural interest in these phenomena has lagged far behind. Nevertheless, something is known about the relationship of such substances to deviance in non-Western societies (see Blum, 1969; Furst, 1972). For one thing, it is almost certain that the use of psychoactive substances is universal. These drugs include, among many others, beer, wine, tobacco, fly agaric, peyote, mescaline, datura, mushrooms, ayahuasca, marijuana, opium, betel nut, coca leaf, kava, and ether. Alcoholic beverages are known from as early as 7000 BC, and opium was known by 2000 BC. These drugs have been used, and misused, for every imaginable (and unimaginable) purpose—from joy, sensuality, and the enhancement of

perception, to degradation, restraint, and the loss of
emotional intensity. For the most part, psychoactive
drugs seem to be used in a culturally appropriate
manner. Sometimes, however, there is trouble.

We have already seen how the Mixtec Indians of
Mexico (Romney & Romney, 1963) attributed the single
act of adult aggression witnessed during the year to
indulgence in alcohol and marijuana. Marlene Dobkin
de Rios (1972) has also described how the use of
ayahuasca in the Peruvian Amazon can lead to adverse
consequences such as acute anxiety or accusations of
witchcraft. Carlos Castaneda's (1968, 1971) detailed
accounts of the use of various psychoactive drugs by
the Yaqui "man of knowledge," Don Juan, show that
such drugs can lead to various kinds of trouble and
to accusations of serious deviance as well as to
knowledge and beauty.

In other societies, the definition of drug usage
as deviant has changed radically over time. "Drug
abuse" is now a major concern in the United States
for well-documented reasons. Many decry the use of
marijuana, the possession of which is a felony in
some states. Others point to the dangers of ampheta-
mines. Drugs such as heroin not only lead to problems
of physical addiction, but also to crime as addicts
are compelled to steal to support their habit.
Garrett O'Connor and his associates (O'Connor, *et al*,
1971) studied opiate addiction in the black ghetto of
Baltimore. They estimated that some 12,000 addicts
lived in this area, and that the annual cost of heroin
for these people was somewhere between $78,000,000 and
$156,000,000. They further estimated that two-thirds
of this cost was borne by the theft of goods (resold
at greatly reduced rates in the community). It should
be clear, then, that heroin addiction is a costly
problem, not only in terms of human misery, but in
dollars and cents as well.

There was a time when opiate addiction was widespread in the United States without being recognized
as a "problem." As H. W. Morgan (1974) reminds us,
before and during the Civil War the use of opiates

was wide spread in all segments of American society.
Children were calmed with opium derivatives, women
used many popular patent medicines which were liber-
ally larded with opiates, and "opium dens" were
probably present in all cities and most towns as
well.   Chloroform, ether, cocaine, and other drugs
were also common.   It was not until after the Civil
War that this pattern of open drug usage was seen as
being sufficiently troublesome to encourage the beginning of legislation against drug abuse, and effective
legislation was not to come for several decades.
    Drug use in a village in northern Rajasthan
illustrates the importance of social and cultural
factors in defining drug usage as deviant (Carstairs,
1954).   In this village the socially important Rajputs
include both the rulers and the warrior caste.   The
drug they choose to use is alcohol, which leads them
to become "boisterous, bawdy, and unbridled."   The
other high caste group in the village, the Brahmins,
denounce the use of alcohol which they see as being
inimical to the religious life they favor.   Instead,
they use bhang *(Cannabis indica)*.   Thus we have the
familiar picture of contrasting social groups in the
same community actively opposed to one another in
their preference for intoxicants.   Should one sub-
culture become dominant, it could well be expected to
take action against the "deviance" of the other.   It
should also be noted that both Rajputs and Brahmins
have rules for the proper use of alcohol or bhang
and each group has its own drug "abusers" whom they
see as being addicts (Carstairs, 1954, p. 225).   To
explain the deviance of these individuals, one would
presumably look to psychological or biological factors.
    The drug about which we have the most extensive
knowledge in non-Western societies is alcohol.   Alcohol provides another example of how psychoactive
substances and deviance may be related.   In many of
the world's societies alcohol is truly "demon rum,"
bringing in its wake terrible mayhem and debauchery.
Yet, people in some societies, such as the Camba
Indians of Bolivia (Heath, 1958), regularly consume

immense quantities of alcohol without displaying any
improper behavior whatsoever. In many other societies
people also drink heavily without allowing their drunkenness to lead to serious trouble. For example, drunken
violence or sexuality may be confined to certain specific occasions or to specific persons, and may occur only
within culturally specified limits (MacAndrew and Edgerton, 1969). The interesting thing about alcohol is that
it often provides an occasion for socially sanctioned
misbehavior. On such occasions, where drunkenness is
accompanied by "changes-for-the-worse"—by violence, sexual impropriety, irresponsibility or the like—it is typically the case that this behavior, which would otherwise be very troublesome, is largely or completely
excused. Such drunken misconduct will still be confined within certain limits, for it is not true that
drunkenness typically is totally "out of control," but
as long as this behavior *is* within the prescribed
limits, even certain kinds of homicide may be excused
(MacAndrew and Edgerton, 1969). "Under the influence"
of alcohol man can sometimes get away with behavior for
which he would ordinarily be punished. Societies may
permit alcohol to remove intention, or agency, from a
man's shoulders, saying that the drug, not he, is at
fault. Societies where alcohol is accorded this
property are a deviant's delight. In such societies,
he is able to "save up" his deviant violence, sexuality, and the like for drunken occasions during which
he may misbehave with relative impunity. Here, we
call attention to man's calculation of the consequences of his deviance and suggest that, to a degree
at least, man is able to deviate when it is most to
his advantage to do so.
    As a case in point, the Pennsylvania Supreme
Court ruled recently (Los Angeles Times, March 26,
1975, p. 16) that a state of "intoxication" or
"drug influence" must be taken into consideration in
determining the intent of a person who commits a crime.
The case at issue involved a burglary-murder by a man
who contended that he had consumed a quart of wine and
taken a "LSD-type pill" and therefore had "no recollec-
tion" of events at the victim's home. His defense

argued that because of his state of intoxication, the
defendant was incapable of forming an intent to commit
burglary.   In what was referred to as "a bitter dis-
sent," three associate justices of the court suggested
"that all a criminal needs now to carry out a successful robbery or burglary would be a revolver in one hand
and a quart of liquor in the other."

Recent cross-cultural research with other psychoactive drugs suggests that these too have the potential
for producing, and excusing, troublesome behavior.
Some of these drugs may also have a potential for reducing deviance (Furst, 1972; Harner, 1973).   Thus, for
example, the use of various tranquilizing drugs may
serve to reduce the incidence of violence in a society.

MENTAL RETARDATION

Mental retardation is another universal phenomenon
with troublemaking potential.   It is important for
illustrative purposes because people who are retarded
do not *intend* to deviate—usually quite the contrary—
but they make trouble nevertheless.   In this regard,
the mentally retarded are like other persons with
physical disabilities such as the deaf, the blind,
or, as we saw earlier, the intersexed.   Mental retardation is not only common (close to 3% of the population in the United States would commonly be diag-
nosed as being mentally retarded), it is particularly
troublesome because it usually occurs in only mild
degree and is therefore by no means totally or even
clearly disabling, nor is it easily identified.

The mildly mentally retarded are deviants in
spite of themselves.   They wish to be *normal* and to
follow the rules of their fellow men but sometimes
they cannot.   The consequences of this inability are
frequently serious, with degradation and even death
being common.   Many mentally retarded people in the
West now receive humane care and treatment but others
continue to be treated with social deprivation and
stigma.   Non-Western societies vary in their response

to the trouble that mentally retarded people pose.
For example, throughout the Arab world, parts of
India, the Himalayas, and parts of Southeast Asia,
the retarded are treated quite well, sometimes even
preferentially. In the Arab countries, such persons
are usually referred to and treated as "saints"
(Ammar, 1954). The Lepchas of Sikkim are also very
understanding of the mentally retarded as Gorer's
(1938, p. 271) account of a retarded man illustrates:

> (The Lepcha) would explain that he was foolish
> and did not know how to behave properly. For
> them this was a sufficient explanation; it
> wasn't his fault he was a fool and this was no
> reason for disliking him, providing he *fulfilled
> his obligations*. (Italics added)

This same point is made in many folk societies, where
it is commonly reported that even the severely retarded are allowed their freedom as long as they are
relatively harmless, but when their ignorance of rules
threatens people, property or decency, they are re-
strained or killed (Edgerton, 1970, pp. 529-530).

Unfortunately, other societies have been far less
tolerant of the trouble posed by retardates. The
Northern Saulteaux Indians thought them to be possessed of devils and burned them alive (Skinner, 1912,
p. 161). The following account by Lamson (1934, p. 389)
of a retarded 20-year-old man amply demonstrates his
difficulties in a Chinese village:

> He was engaged early by his parents. Before his
> marriage he asked village people to teach him how
> to talk with his wife when he saw her, and what to
> call his mother-in-law. People were very glad to
> play tricks on him . . . a large crowd gathered
> before his home to see the funny wedding.

Lamson goes on to tell us that after marriage he was
treated cruelly and forced to do hard domestic tasks.
His in-laws gave him little food and only second-hand
clothing, and "repeatedly beat him with sticks."

Even on easy-going Samoa, Margaret Mead reports
that the life of a retarded girl, Sala, was anything
but pleasant (1949, p. 122).

> She was stupid, underhanded, deceitful and she
> possessed no aptitude for the simplest mechani-
> cal tasks. Her ineptness was the laughing stock
> of the village . . . It was a saying among the
> girls of the village that Sala was apt at only
> one art, sex, and that she, who couldn't even
> sew thatch or weave blinds, would never get a
> husband.

Mead reports that the attitude towards her was one of
contempt, and that Sala knew it only too well.

Jean Briggs' (1970) sensitive account of Nigi,
a mildly retarded Eskimo woman, is poignant indeed.
This woman's confused speech, girlish giggles, clumsy
motions, and general incompetence made her the target
of scorn and criticism. She was usually criticized
behind her back, however, not to her face. In the
Greek village of Vasilika the abuse is more open.
Children in Vasilika are teased and ridiculed until
they learn how to behave in an appropriate way. But
mentally retarded individuals are said never to
learn, so they are baited and teased all their lives
for the amusement of those who watch and laugh
(Friedl, 1964, p. 79).

It is apparent that societies differ in their
response to mental retardation. But even when there
is clearly no intent involved, retarded persons
sometimes damage property, fail to display the required social attributes or propriety, or otherwise
disappoint, offend, or frighten. As such they are
troublemakers and are sometimes dealt with harshly.

The causes of mental retardation in folk societies, as in the United States, are various and, except
for certain biological causes such as infection,
genetic anomaly, or hypoxia at birth, they can seldom
be determined with certainty. The most relevant
issue here is not what causes mental retardation—or
blindness, or any other physical disability—but why
some cultures regard it as seriously troublesome and

others do not. About this subject, we remain almost
wholly ignorant.

MENTAL ILLNESS

Mental illness is an omnibus concept that embraces
various disturbances of thought, emotion, and behavior.
The presence of such disturbances, mild and severe
alike, is now generally agreed to be universal. As a
working definition, one may speak of mental illness
when a person's thoughts, emotions, or behaviors appear to others in his society to be unreasonable or
irrational, or when his ability to cope with the ordinary demands of life is impaired. Returning to our
earlier discussion of an account, a person is often
defined as being mentally ill when he is unable to
give—or to have given for him—an account that adequately explains his apparent irrationality. Thus,
a person who attempts to account for his troublesome behavior by insisting that voices told him how
to behave or that he is indeed Jesus Christ, is
likely, in our society, to be labeled mentally ill.
People who are seen, or labeled, as mentally ill are
likely to undergo a distinct change in their moral
and jural status, usually involving a reduction of
rights and responsibilities. As a recent study by
Rosenhan (1973) has dramatically emphasized, mental
illness is difficult to diagnose, but once it has
been labeled, the result—at least in psychiatric institutions in the United States—can be a self-fulfill-
ing prophecy. Rosenhan had various professionals
enter mental hospitals by complaining that they were
hearing voices. Once they were admitted, as they all
were, they behaved normally but could convince no one
on the psychiatric staff that the original diagnoses
were incorrect, although fellow patients often recognized these people for the "pseudo-patients" they really
were. The deviant label of mental illness, like so many
others, may be so difficult to escape because it
identifies a person who may be potentially troublesome,

even though he may not intend to be. Although mental
illness may be examined by means of any or all of the
five perspectives mentioned earlier, it is used here
to illustrate the process of labeling as it is related to asking for and giving an account.

Sometimes mental illness may be chronic and
severe, and thus recognized by all, but still not be
very troublesome. Such a circumstance is illustrated
by an elderly Sebei man of Uganda who had for some
years spent most of his waking hours hanging upside
down from the limb of a tree or a rafter in his house.
His only comments were: "I have a chicken in my
head," or "I have countless wives." Most Sebei
easily agreed in labeling him psychotic. Yet he
troubled no one outside his family and he was in turn
left undisturbed (Edgerton 1969, p. 56). Other
forms of mental illness may occur only occasionally
but nevertheless be very troublesome indeed, as in the
Malaysian *amok* in which a passerby may be attacked, or
the Ojibwa *witiko* in which an unfortunate victim may
not only be killed, but eaten as well (Parker, 1960).

In folk societies as well as in the West, the
consequences of mental illness, and the deviant label
itself, are often negotiable. I have reported cases
from East Africa where psychotic behavior was used to
personal advantage, and other instances where apparently flagrant psychotic behavior was not labeled
as such because there were compelling reasons not to
do so (Edgerton, 1969). It is this latter phenomenon—
turning the label of mental illness to one's advantage—that I would like to emphasize. A deviant label
is frequently something that one disavows when asked
for an account, but it is sometimes actively sought for
the advantage it confers.

A paradigm for this sort of phenomenon may
be found in the widespread occurrence of what has
been called *possession hysteria* throughout the world.
An excellent account of such behavior—*saka*—among the
Taita of Kenya (Harris, 1957) illustrates the phenomenon and the social circumstances that bring it about.
Among the Taita, men thoroughly dominate women, who

respond by expressing their dissatisfaction in various ways. One such expression is saka, a classical
form of possession hysteria marked by convulsive
movements, monotonous acts, speaking in tongues, and
apparent dissociation. Only women are possessed by
the spirits that give rise to an attack of saka.
Women so possessed either fear or desire male things.
Thus they may dress and dance as a male, temporarily
but realistically taking over the male role. But
women may also appear to be hysterical and demand
that men for once give them what they desire,
usually material goods. Since saka is thought to be
a dangerous illness, one which can result in death,
men comply with these demands. Harris notes that
some women who have saka attacks appear to be genu-
inely overcome with anxiety or hysteria. Thus, the
authenticity of the "illness" is demonstrated to
all. On the other hand, Harris also notes that some
women engage in pretense, falsely claiming a privilege which the legitimate illness of other women has
made possible.

There are also intriguing accounts of so-called
"hysterical" behavior in the New Guinea highlands.
Among the Gururumba, a man who manifests controlled
violence and property destruction (like that of a
"wild pig") may be seen as a "wild man," labeled psychotic, and consequently permitted by others to
escape from the press of economic and social responsibilities (Newman, 1964). Newman says that there are
no sanctions against a wild man after he has "gone
wild," and that no one in his clan or village will
mention the episode to him. They will talk about it
among themselves, however, and these conversations
make it clear that people do not think of him as the
same man he was before the "wild man" episode. In
Newman's words: "the wild man does not become an
outcast or deviant in the eyes of others; he becomes a man now known to be incapable of, or unwilling
to participate in, certain affairs with the same degree of intensity as others, but still a man who can
participate to some degree" (1964, p. 17).

Similar behavior occurs among the nearby Bena Bena (this sort of episode has been reported for many societies in the highlands of New Guinea), but here the wild man is not permitted to escape his social obligations (Langness, 1965a). A hard-pressed Gururumba man can escape certain onerous economic obligations without losing all his rights in other aspects of life; a Bena Bena cannot. Thus we see once again that the same kind of phenomenon may be variously responded to by different societies, just as it may be variously motivated, and excused, within the same society.

Chapter 4

The Folk Urban Distinction and Deviance

The foregoing introduction to various kinds of troublesome, or potentially troublesome, behavior has illustrated several of the phenomena relevant to any cross-cultural perspective on "deviance." It also attempted to clarify the "folk-urban" assumptions about deviance. Obviously, other categories of deviance could have been included. For example, witchcraft beliefs and practices are very troublesome in many of the world's societies, but are relatively unimportant in the West; conversely, child abuse is a tragically troublesome form of deviance in the West, but is relatively uncommon in folk societies. Although these and other similar forms of deviance were not discussed here, the eight categories of deviance that were presented should provide an adequate introduction to the issues we have raised. Before turning to the more general considerations, let us look again at the folk-urban issue.

      The first, and most incontestable, observation to be made is that the existing ethnographic literature does not provide the data that would permit us to make any quantitative comparison between folk and urban societies with regard to deviance. Whether the comparison is based on a continuum of simplicity to complexity or on socio-economic types (e.g., hunters and gatherers, pastoralists, peasants, etc.),

we must admit that the available data are inadequate
for quantitative analysis. For example, it is apparent that troublemaking based on self-interest occurs
in all societies. It is also apparent that the frequency of such troublemaking differs from one society
to another, but just how it differs or how much we
cannot say. What we can say with confidence is that
folk societies are not as free of deviance as either
Redfield's heuristic theory or the conventional
wisdom would predict. Empirical evidence from various sources has long been accumulating that fails
to support the ideal folk type proposed by Redfield.
For one thing, it is apparent that no society has
ever held all of its members strictly accountable
for all of their actions so that each and every
breach of a rule carried with it inevitable or
identical punishment. Instead, we find that in
folk societies, as in our own, rules are often very
fuzzy around the edges—they are relative to the situation, the actor and the audience, and they leave
substantial room for disagreement and negotiation
about what is or is not just and proper.

For example, Embree (1950, p.182) wrote this
about village life in Thailand: "The first charac-
teristic of Thai culture to strike an observer from
the West, or from Japan or Vietnam, is the individualistic behavior of the people. The longer one
resides in Thailand the more one is struck by the
almost determined lack of regularity, discipline
and regimentation in Thai life." The Kamba of
Kenya have been characterized by their avoidance
of specificity in many of their cultural principles:
"The rules are often vague and open-ended. They
tend to be quite general, and a person is expected
to make his own interpretation of them. The 'right
thing' to do *should* emerge from argument and discussion, and the argument, though loosely structured, is
by no means predetermined" (Oliver, 1965, p.427).

Examples such as these that reflect the ambiguity of cultural rules are found throughout the

literature on folk societies of the world. The
Pygmies of the Ituri forest in the Congo often argue
over their culture, with agreement often being far
too much to hope for (Turnbull, 1961); the Paliyans
of South India, a small and isolated society, display a truly monumental lack of agreement concerning
many of their cultural norms, apparently achieving
relative consensus only where rules concerning violence are at issue (Gardner, 1966, p.898). Similar
examples abound, as, for example,from Choiseul in
Melanesia (Scheffler, 1965), Ceylon (Leach, 1961),
village India (Beals, 1967), in pre-industrial
England (Laslett, 1965) or a modern English village
(Blythe, 1969).

Members of folk societies are not slaves to
their customs. Their customs are often quite flexible, and this flexibility may result in a wide
range of acceptable behavior. Indeed, in reviewing
26 hunting and gathering societies around the world,
Peter Gardner (1966, p. 409) concluded: "The very
extreme individualism found among food gathering
tribes contrasts with the lesser individualism
of so-called individualistic complex societies."
In fact, in some very small societies the expression
of individual variability in conduct can become so
pronounced that the discovery of rules becomes very
difficult indeed. It is this point that Levi-Strauss
(1961, p. 310) makes when he says of the Nambikwara,
a small South American society, "The society of the
Nambikwara had been reduced to the point at which
I found nothing but human beings."

Hunters and gatherers, then, who often live in
man's smallest, simplest, and most isolated societies, do not behave as "folk" should. Along with
the Siriono, Redfield would have to exclude hunters
and gatherers from the folk type. It is possible
to argue that Redfield would be correct in doing so,
since many hunting and gathering societies may be
somewhat disorganized fragments of larger and better
organized societies that have been forced to eke out
a living in marginal environments by emphasizing

flexible and individualistic survival skills. In
this view, true "folk" societies would be found
among larger communities living in areas that provide better subsistence. The trouble with this
position is that these larger, more settled and
better-fed folk societies do not behave like
Redfield's *folk* either. The Mbuti Pygmies, for
example, are hunters and gatherers but their subsistence base is good; so it is with the Bushmen.
In both societies, however, there is notable individualism as well as deviance. Note that our
earlier examples of cultural flexibility were drawn
from settled, food-producing people (Thailand and
the Kamba of Kenya). Many of the examples of
deviant behavior presented earlier were taken from
folk societies (e.g., Azande, Gusii, Kapauku Papuans,
Tikopia), which cannot be construed as disorganized
social fragments that have been forced to adopt
individualistic behavior in order to survive in
inhospitable environments.
 Supporters of Redfield's folk theory might
grant all this and yet argue that societies such as
the ones exemplified here show individualism and
deviance as a result of European acculturation and
subsequent colonial presence. While it is undeniably the case that acculturation has long been
universal (recently contacted relict populations
such as the Tasadays of the Philippines are so rare
an exception that for all practical purposes it is
correct to say that true isolation is a fiction)
and the influence of state governments is widespread,
it would not seem reasonable that such European
influence can be made to account for all of the
deviance we have reported. Here we encounter a
crucial weakness in the ideal folk type. It may
be reasonable to contrast *folk* with *urban* on
a criterion of relative isolation, but it is not
reasonable to attribute the deviance present in
actual folk societies primarily to social and cultural changes brought about by contacts with other
societies. Such contacts have occurred throughout

history and are an inevitable accompaniment of life in folk as well as urban societies. If the folk concept is to have any utility, it must incorporate the presence of acculturation. The more reasonable question is whether the deviance reported in folk societies is the result of social disorganization brought about by the recent impact of Western technology and political domination. There is no conclusive answer to this question. It is undeniably true that Western influence has been both widespread and subtle, but it would nevertheless appear that the societies mentioned earlier reflect a wide range of experience with Western influence yet *all* have deviance. Moreover, societies that have been dramatically changed by Westernization have not been used here.

It should also be noted that some anthropologists have explicitly denied that the diversity and deviance they have recorded in folk societies are recent phenomena related to socio-cultural change. The Walbiri, Australian aborigines of the Central Desert, illustrate this point. The Walbiri are clearly *folk* by Redfield's criteria, but their social organization is anything but simple, as M. J. Meggitt points out. Meggitt notes that deviance, with regard to appropriate marriage partners, for example, did occur but that such deviations from the norms did not greatly bother the Walbiri. This anomalous behavior was eventually made to fit into the framework of Walbiri culture. What is more, Meggitt notes that these discrepancies "are not a recent product of social disorganization following European contact; the very complexity of Walbiri social structure made it inevitable that there would always be some individuals who could not, or would not, follow all the rules" (Meggitt, 1962, p. 219).

Sometimes members of folk cultures themselves make the same point. In studying Choiseul, in the Solomon Islands, Scheffler found that when actual behavior did not conform to "custom," as it often

did not, various Choiseulese would blame this deviance on modern influences. But eventually, "more
knowledgeable informants" convinced him that deviations from custom were part of the past as well as
the present, saying: "Our customs have never been
firm . . .We look only for that which will help us
live well, and the rest is just talk" (1965, p. 112).

Western influence on deviant behavior should
never be discounted. Each individual society
requires careful analysis. However, caution should
be taken not to assume that Western socio-cultural
influence is necessarily behind all deviance. There
is too much evidence to indicate that deviance in
folk societies cannot so easily be explained away.
The theory of folk society which assumes that such
societies are without deviance is nowhere approx-
imated by the realities of life in existing folk
societies.

The validity of the *urban* type in the *folk-urban*
comparison has also been called into question. Historians Henri Pirenne (1956) and Marc Bloch (1961)
have pointed out that Medieval cities in Europe were
by no means alike, and Sylvia Thrupp (1966) has
called attention to the fact that European cities
were long seen not as centers of deviance but as
bastians of order against the barbarians or armed
enemies who brought disorder to the countryside.
Recently, Emilio Willems (1970) has documented the
folk character of the German city, Cologne, showing
that there is a continuity, not a polarity, between
the urban lower class and the peasantry.

Asian cities, too, sometimes fail to take on
the character required of them by folk-urban theory.
For example, the anthropologist, Edward Bruner,
concluded that, contrary to the traditional folk-
urban theory, many Asian cities have not become
secularized, the individual has not become isolated,
kinship organizations have not broken down, and
social relationships have not become impersonal,
superficial, and utilitarian. "It is clear that

the social concomitants of the transition from rural
to urban life are not the same in Southeast Asia as
in Western society, but why this should be so is not
entirely clear" (Bruner, 1961, p. 508).

It is also not entirely clear that Western urban
society always follows this pattern either. To be
sure, we are familiar with urban alienation and
crime, but we also possess accounts of *folk* enclaves
in the most urban of Western cities (Mangin, 1970).
Even in the largest American and European cities
there are neighborhoods, barrios, gangs, and the
like, that retain the attributes Redfield reserved
for *small and isolated* societies. These are *communities*, and within them there is often no evidence
of conspicuous social disorganization or rule violation. There is deviance in all cities, but not
all cities, or even all parts of the same city, can
be shown to have more deviance than is found in some
so-called *folk* societies.

Perhaps the best that we can say about the folk-urban continuum as an explanation of deviance is
that it often fails to find support either from the
study of small and isolated societies or from large
urban ones. We are left with this observation:
troublesome behavior is frequent and varied in the
world's small and simple societies. It is so frequent and so varied, in fact, that there is no reason
to believe that deviant behavior is wholly or even
largely a product of urban living. An explanation
of human deviance must be sought in less simplistic
terms.

What must shape the nature of our inquiry is
this: *deviance occurs in all societies*. It occurs
in the small as well as the large, the simple as well
as the complex. Deviance may take different forms
and frequencies from one society to another, but
deviance is ubiquitous. What David Matza has said
of Western society appears to be true for any society:
". . .deviant phenomena are common and natural. They
are a normal and inevitable part of social life, as
is their denunciation, regulation, and prohibition"

(1969, p. 13). If deviance is an ever-present fact of human existence, as it appears to be, how might we explain it?

Chapter 5

Understanding Deviance

One of the few things that everyone agrees upon is
that explanation in the social sciences is a complex
and difficult undertaking. As the years pass, con-
troversies over present or future success in explaining human behavior seem to become more, not less,
heated. Those who contend that explanation can take
the same form in the social sciences as that which
has been successful in the physical sciences admit
that human behavior is complex, that humans react
against efforts to study them, and that the social
sciences are still inexperienced. Nevertheless,
they believe that it is possible to assemble evidence and control possible causes until the most
likely one is discovered. The resulting *explanation*
would be probabilistic, to be sure, but an explanation that accounts for 60% or 70% of the cases of
suicide or homicide would be valuable indeed.

Opponents believe that such goals are unattain-
able and that claims of success are illusory. Those
who take this position argue that the most reasonable
goal is not the explanation of behavior that might
lead to the discovery of laws of human behavior, but
the understanding of a particular instance of human
behavior in its social and cultural context. Philosopher A. R. Louch (1966) has persuasively contended
that human behavior—deviant or not—must be understood
as essentially moral, as a product of motives, values,

and intentions that together are seen by all concerned as good or bad, right or wrong. In this view,
the study of accounts would be appropriate, but the
effort to explain deviant behavior in terms of
"social strain" or "subcultural conflict" would
be ill-advised. For those who agree that anthropology's primary task is the understanding of complexity
in its own right, not the reduction of complexity to
simplicity, the words of Clifford Geertz (1973, p. 29)
are especially apt:

> Cultural analysis is intrinsically incomplete.
> And, worse than that, the more deeply it goes,
> the less complete it is. It is a strange
> science whose most telling assertions are its
> most tremulously based, in which to get some-
> where with the matter at hand is to intensify
> the suspicion, both your own and that of others,
> that you are not getting it right.

Any effort here to resolve these opposing points
of view would be pointless. It is more profitable
to assume that whether one is attempting to *explain*
or to *understand*, we still have a great deal to learn
about deviant behavior and either perspective can
contribute to that process of learning.

The examples of deviance in folk societies
presented earlier could have been organized differ-
ently. Instead of being grouped by categories of
deviance (e.g., violence, mental illness), they
could have been presented under the most relevant
form of explanation (e.g., social strain, subcultural conflict, etc.). But such an organization
would have encouraged two mistakes. First, it would
have contributed to a false sense of certainty concerning which explanation provides the best understanding of the deviance in question, because explanations of deviance can rarely be assigned with much
confidence. What is more, such an organization
would have observed a major point—cultural variability. The most incontestable conclusion that can be
reached with regard to deviant behavior is that

societies differ significantly in the amount and
type of deviance that occurs within them. Thus,
if one wants to understand a deviant act—how it
came about, what its consequences will be, and
whether it is likely to recur—one must first
understand the culture of the society in which
it occurs. This is not only true for an understanding of a single deviant act in any given
society, it is equally true of a class of deviance,
such as suicide, in various societies. Therefore,
our attention is returned to accounts—to the ways
in which people get into and out of trouble—and
how these ways differ from culture to culture.
We begin, then, with culture, but we should not
stop there. To do so would forfeit any hope of a
more general understanding of deviance. The five
explanations offered in Chapter One can sharpen
and expand our understanding. They may even lead
to an understanding which transcends cultural
specifics and applies to deviant behavior in any
society. In a sense, then, cultural analysis is
always necessary, but sometimes not sufficient,
for an understanding of deviance.

Thus far, the effort to explain man's deviance
has centered on the study of his social and cultural environment. Since the social sciences are
social and cultural by choice, it is not surprising that they have sought the sources of deviant
behavior in man's socio-cultural environment.
What is more, the psychological study of deviance
has also emphasized these same environmental
circumstances (Zigler, 1970). This emphasis is
clearly reflected in the five explanations that
were introduced earlier. The ones most commonly
used are environmental: social-strain, subcultural conflict, and psychological defense or
commitment.

Although these environmental theories were
developed to explain deviance in the complex urban
societies of the West, it should be obvious, that
they can also be applied to small and simple

societies. For example, we have seen that social
strain theory need not be reserved for disorganized,
swiftly changing or class-stratified societies. It
can be applied as well in stable, well-integrated
societies whose only stratification is by age, sex,
or ability. The generational conflict of the Samburu
is an example, as is the homosexuality of the Azande,
and the homicide in Teklum. Similarly, we need not
look to ethnically diverse cities to find subcultural
difference and conflict at work. Subcultural conflicts based on age are central to the deviance
exhibited by Samburu warriors, and subcultural conflict among the Azande is based on sex as is homicide in Teklum. So it is with the psychological
explanations. Evidence of psychological defense and
commitment is abundantly present in the troublemaking behavior of people in the smallest, simplest
and most homogeneous societies we know.

It is clear, then, that the major environmental
explanations are *relevant* to deviance in any kind of
society. What is not so clear is just how well they
explain deviance in *any* society. It is true that
deviant behavior can be construed in terms of these
explanations and that doing so can be helpful to
the social analyst. The rub enters when any given
deviant case is offered for explanation. Then it
becomes clear, as in the case of Cephu, that *all*
these explanations can be made to apply, and that
even biological explanations cannot be ruled out.
We always lack crucial information and are consequently forced to conclude that many factors seem
to be operative and few can be ruled out altogether.
Therefore it is proper to interject a cautionary note
by saying that while most social scientists believe
that man's deviant behavior, like his conforming behavior, is determined primarily by his social and
cultural environment, this position is contestable.
We have yet to demonstrate this point conclusively
by a series of empirical studies; and we have not
clarified the conceptual issues that are involved
in such studies. As a result, we must admit the

possibility that deviant behavior may also be determined by man's biology, either normal or defective.

This may seem to be a reasonable, even middle-
of-the-road, declaration, but it is neither self-
evident nor fully acceptable to many anthropologists,
sociologists, and psychologists who continue to focus
their research on environmental determinants of
deviance. Environmental determinism found its most
extreme statement in the behaviorism of Watson:

> Give me a dozen healthy infants, well-formed,
> and my own specified world to bring them up,
> and I'll guarantee to take any one at random
> and train him to become any type of specialist
> I might select—doctor, lawyer, artist, merchant,
> and yes, even beggar and thief, regardless of
> the talents, penchants, tendencies, abilities,
> vocations, and race of his ancestors. (1925,
> p. 218)

Most modern students of the environment are not quite
so cavalier in their disregard of behavior genetics,
but their emphasis nevertheless remains on the extraordinary plasticity of human behavior and, consequently, on the ways in which man's environment molds
his behavior.

Except for dyed-in-the-wool behaviorists, most
behavioral scientists today are interactionists,
meaning that they see any human behavior as a result
of inherited biological factors in interaction with
environmental ones. This is a perfectly acceptable
position in view of our present knowledge, for we
believe that genetic or extragenetic inheritance is
profoundly influenced by both pre natal and perinatal factors as well as by all of the influences
encountered throughout life. It is known, for example, that even such autonomic nervous system
functions as heart rate, EEG, and blood pressure
can be modified by instrumental and classical con-
ditioning (DiCara, 1970). In many cases, however,
investigators interested in deviant behavior will
nod appreciatively to biological considerations

and to interactionism as a perspective, only to
declare that biological matters cannot yet be studied
adequately. They then turn their full attention to
environmental considerations. It is quite correct
that there are serious difficulties in assessing
biological determinants of deviant behavior, but
it should also be recognized that difficulties of
comparable magnitude confront anyone who concentrates
solely on the social and cultural environment.

Without in any way implying that environmental
factors are not of great significance (we have, you
will recall, said that culture is of overriding significance), let us see what can be added to our
understanding of deviance by looking also at various
biological factors. If we think in terms of statistical variance, let us ask how much of the variance
in deviant behavior can be accounted for by biological factors?

Chapter 6

Biological Factors in
Deviant Behavior

Due to rapid advances in such fields as behavior
genetics, biochemistry and neurophysiology, efforts
to account for deviant behavior by means of biological defect or damage are becoming more credible each
year. Advances in genetic theory and deviant behavior are particularly impressive. While many investigators are not yet willing to agree with Rosenthal's
(1971) polygenic theory that all mental illness and
perhaps all deviance may have a genetic basis, evidence for the heritability of various disorders is
increasing. Some afflictions such as PKU (Phenyl-
ketonuria), are obviously inherited, with monozygotic
twins (MZ) being 100% concordant, which means that all
such twins would develop the disorder regardless of
environmental conditions. Down's syndrome (Mongolism)
has a concordance rate that is almost 100%. Depres-
sion is now known to take two forms (bipolar or manic-
depressive, and unipolar or simply depressive) and
both appear to have large genetic components, as does
schizophrenia. Concordance rates for this latter disorder vary from one study to the next (difficulties
in diagnosing the condition reliably are well known).
It appears to be the case, however, that the more
severe the expression of schizophrenia, the more
clear-cut is its inheritance (Rosenthal, 1970,
p. 122). Personality attributes such as anxiety,
inhibition, introversion-extroversion, etc., also

appear to have some genetic basis. Evidence for the
heritability of overt forms of deviance such as
"criminality" or alcoholism is still highly equivocal
(Slater and Cowie, 1971).

    In evaluating genetic interpretations, we should
recognize that new information requiring the revision
of existing theories can be expected to appear. For
example, geneticists have studied diabetes for many
years and even though the genetics are complex, most
geneticists conclude that diabetes has a significant
genetic component because it occurs with dispropor-
tionate frequency among family members. Various
studies of co-twins indicated that MZ twins had
concordance rates for clinical diabetes that ranged
from 38% to as much as 73% depending on the severity
of the symptoms or the age of onset. This is not a
clear-cut picture to be sure, but since there was no
viable theory of contagion for diabetes, these findings pointed to a major genetic component in diabetes.
The genetic findings regarding diabetes have been
likened to those for schizophrenia because of their
complexity, the possibility that both represent the
tail on a normal distribution curve and their sensi-
tivity to environmental factors (Vandenberg, 1968).
Students of deviant behavior should take notice,
therefore, when it is reported (Maugh, 1975) that
epidemiological research shows a possible viral
etiology for diabetes. That is, a theory of contagion has now been seriously proposed. This finding
need not suggest that schizophrenia also has a viral
cause, but rather that mental illness like schizophrenia, which may have a genetic component, might
be a product of complicated gene-environment inter-
actions, the nature of which we have yet to fully
comprehend. There are many difficulties that relate
to the study of the genetics of human behavior. It
is only reasonable to conclude, however, that some
individuals more than others may inherit a genotypic
predisposition to behave in ways that will lead them
to the expression of behaviors which other people
will judge as deviant. We shall return to this possibility when we discuss temperament.

There are non-genetic biological factors to be
considered as well. For example, there is growing
evidence for the deleterious effect of poor nutrition
on intellectual development. Thus, Zamenhof (1971)
has reported that the offspring of protein-deprived
pregnant rats suffer not only a marked loss of brain
cells, but general systemic damage as well, particularly involving an inability to utilize protein
even when it is abundant in the diet. Evidence concerning the effect of poor nutrition on human populations is also accumulating (Cravioto, 1968; Birch and
Gussow, 1970), while Wallace and his colleagues have
linked calcium deficiency to mental illness (Katz and
Foulks, 1970; Wallace, 1972). Similarly, evidence is
increasingly available that suggests links between
hormonal imbalance to deviant behavior. For example,
Green (1972) has linked imbalance in sex hormones to
homosexuality and aggressive behavior.
    Other investigators have studied the brain in
relationship to violence. The assumption is made
that all behavior is filtered through the central
nervous system, and that certain people who have
difficulty controlling their violent impulses do so
because of a malfunctioning brain mechanism. Mark
and Ervin (1970) have reported that there are brain
mechanisms for controlling violence and when these
are not functioning correctly, impulsive violence
is the result. Such controls are said to be located
in the limbic system, particularly in the amygdala.
These authors report that removal or ablation of the
damaged amygdala in violent patients has been successful in controlling violent behavior. Others
have challenged this position, arguing that brain
mechanisms such as those thought to be involved in
the inhibition or control of aggression are not as
localized as Mark and Ervin believe but are instead
widely dispersed throughout the brain. An interesting
review of brain and behavior relevant to deviance is
available in Valenstein (1973). In addition, the
noted neuroscientist, John Eccles (1973), has provided an introduction to brain functioning that should
be essential reading for students of deviant behavior.

Others have emphasized the role of birth injury in deviant behavior. Mednick (1970), for example, has pointed to serious birth complications as a possible cause of schizophrenia. Mednick found that anoxia at birth may damage the hippocampus, reducing its ability to inhibit the secretion of ACTH, thus leading to hyper-arousal of the nervous system, a condition that he believes to be central in schizophrenia. His theory is an alternative to a genetic explanation of schizophrenia.

Investigators in many other areas of biological research have reported equally relevant findings. Some, like Rosenthal (1971) or Rimland (1969), see biological defects as primary causes of certain kinds of deviant behavior. Others, such as Werner and her colleagues (1971), who have studied perinatal stress in Hawaii, conclude that while biological factors can indeed account for physical disability and/or behavioral deviance, environmental stress is a far more potent cause of deviance. It may well prove to be correct that most forms of deviant behavior can be better explained by causes related to man's environment rather than to his biology. However, the list of deviant behaviors that *can* in large part be accounted for by biological factors is growing in length and in credibility.

It is increasingly apparent that we limit our ability to understand deviance if we fail to recognize that man's capacity to adapt to his environment—including his ability to understand and follow rules—is influenced by his biology. The influence of any environment on man's behavior must be filtered through man's brain, and any response is then carried out by the rest of his body. Certain men may perform certain deviant acts at certain times because they are biologically predisposed to do so—by their genetic constitution, by their exposure to prenatal or perinatal stress, by poor early nutrition, or by the toxins, diseases and injuries encountered throughout life.

Chapter 7
Temperament and Deviance

The conclusion we drew from our consideration of
deviant biology was that some men may be less able
or less willing than others to live trouble-free
lives because of biological defect or damage. This
is an incomplete statement of the phenomenon, for
the same thing may be said about men with perfectly
normal, but atypical, biology. Thus, our attention
is directed to temperamental individuality. Temperament refers to an individual's genetic predisposition to react to an environment in certain ways.
Individuals are found to differ in their moods,
rhythms, irritabilities, reaction times, energy
levels, frustration tolerance, and the like, and
these differences are present in early infancy.
Temperamental differences are an important and
often neglected source of trouble in human affairs.
     That human individuality was present in the
simplest of societies was emphasized by Franz Boas,
the founder of anthropology in America, and by Radin
(1927) and others. The presence of such diversity
was also acknowledged in Benedict's configurationist
theory even though this theory was instrumental in
discounting the importance of temperamental differences. As you will recall, Benedict (1934) believed
that such differences were inborn, but were sufficiently susceptible to environmental molding that

all but a handful of individuals could fit their
temperaments to the demands of their society.
Benedict's influential theory was followed by the
equally important work of Margaret Mead in her book,
Sex and Temperament in Three Primitive Societies
(1935). This controversial book conveyed the idea
that temperamental differences between the sexes are
a product of culture, not biology. There is evidence
to suggest that Mead herself was long aware of the
importance of temperamental differences and did not
intend to issue quite so categorical a rejection of
temperamental factors in behavior, but the message
of her book was generally taken to be a categorical
rejection of biology nevertheless (Mead, 1972).

Perhaps as a result, temperamental, or "consti-
tutional," determinants of personality have rarely
received much attention from anthropologists concerned with either normal or abnormal personality
(Singer, 1961).   The realization that individual
differences exist in every society was often ignored
(Lindesmith and Strauss, 1950), or if such differences were noted, the sources of these differences
were not typically attributed to variations in temperament   (Kluckhohn, Murray, and Schneider, 1955,
p. 57).

The neglect of temperament in anthropology continued into the 1960s despite the presence of such
perplexing reports as that of C. W. M. Hart (1954)
about five Australian brothers from the Tiwi tribe
of Melville and Bathurst Islands, North Australia.
These five men all had the same mother, although
three had one father, and two had another. Hart's
contention was that since all five were socialized
by the same mother in a small aboriginal society
that was not tolerant of deviance, all five should
be very much alike—if, that is, the social and cultural environment were the dominant force in molding
personality. Instead, the five brothers were remarkably different, spanning an extraordinary range of
personality attributes. Hart concluded that these
differences were temperamental in origin. Hart's

report supporting temperamental determinants of personality had remarkably little influence, however;
it has remained for investigators outside of anthropology to pursue the relationship between deviance
and temperament. Morris Opler (1964) and Eliot
Chapple (1970) are exceptions who have been concerned
with temperament although not with its relationship
to deviant behavior.

About the same time that Hart wrote, the bio-
chemist Roger J. Williams (1956) took issue with
prevailing ideas about biological individuality. He
noted that it was a commonly accepted point of view
in such fields as biology, physiology, biochemistry,
psychology, medicine, and psychiatry, to divide
humanity into two groups: the "vast majority" who
possess biological attributes within the normal range,
and a "small minority" who possess biological attributes "far enough out of line so that they should be
considered deviates" (1956, p. 2).

Williams examined the evidence for such a
biological division between people and found it to
be lacking. He reported great variations among
clinically *normal* people in nerves, muscles, tendons,
bones, blood, organ weights, endocrine-gland weights,
etc. Turning to differences in hormonal levels
which may be significant in deviant behavior, he
reported that each individual person whether "normal"
or not, apparently ". . .must have a distinctive
endocrine pattern which is based upon the anatomical
and physiological potentialities of each gland and
the intricate balances which exist between the different endocrine agents. The distinctiveness of
these patterns involves differences in single items
not of the order of 10, 20, or 50 percent, but often
differences of as much as 10-fold or more" (1956,
p. 95). Williams goes on to say that the concept of
normal which predominates in medicine should be
replaced by the hypothesis that everyone is a deviant,
an idea that should make both therapy and prophylaxis
more effective.

Other investigators were noting the presence, and possible significance, of marked individual differences in infants, even in newborns (Escalona, 1968; Westman, 1973). Such differences are presumably largely genetic, although some could be due to prenatal or perinatal factors. The relevance of such differences to the understanding of deviant behavior has also been studied. Thomas, Chess, and Birch (1968) began to study a cohort of 136 children from 85 families in New York in 1956. They observed the children, interviewed their parents and teachers, and made various measures of temperament. These measures, which began in infancy and were repeated throughout the study, included activity level, rhythmicity, adaptability, distractibility, intensity of reaction, quality of mood, etc. There were marked differences in temperamental traits among the 136 children, but the pattern of traits for any individual child proved to be remarkably stable for that child over the 12 years of research.

Two important clusters of temperamental traits were noted in these children. One cluster was marked by irregularity, negative mood, excessive persistence, distractibility, and the like. Children with this cluster of traits were "difficult" to raise and their temperaments were negatively evaluated by their parents, teachers, etc. The other pattern was "positive," including such attributes as regularity, a positive approach to new stimuli, adaptability to change, and the like. Children with this cluster of traits were seen as being easy to raise. At the time of the report, 12 years later, 42 of the 136 children had developed "behavior problems" as defined by behavioral symptoms and psychiatric evaluations. Of the so-called "difficult" children, 70% had developed such problems, but only 18% of the "easy" children had done so.

In addition to these striking findings, the investigators recorded a developmental sequence of considerable interest for those interested in understanding deviance. They assumed that temperamental traits such as those listed earlier were neutral. All of these children, that is, were potentially normal. Their temperamental traits became good or bad, *difficult* or *easy* only as others (parents, siblings, teachers) came to see them as such. In the culture to which these particular children belonged, some traits were seen as being undesirable, and most children (70%) with such patterns of temperament became deviants. Very few children (18%) with traits seen as being desirable became deviant. Thomas *et al*. (1968) have given us reason to restate Benedict's configurational model as follows: (1) children are born temperamentally diverse; (2) the vast majority cannot easily be molded to the cultural ideal; (3) no one is really *molded* at all, because temperament is largely unyielding to cultural pressure; (4) depending in part on their abilities and motivations, those who possess culturally favored traits are relatively unlikely to become deviant, but those with undesirable traits are very likely to do so.

This formulation is preliminary and requires research by other investigators. Its importance lies in the fact that it suggests the important relationship of temperament to behavior. People *are* born with varying patterns of temperament, and these patterns *are* relatively difficult to change. Societies can easily choose to define some patterns of temperament as bad and others as good. The process is a classic example of labeling theory, with secondary deviance resulting from the imposition of a deviant label. This perspective adds that the "primary" deviance—for example, hyperactivity—can be biological, something over which a child (or an adult) may have little control.

We should take note of the possibility that deviance may not only be a product of biological defect or anomaly, but that it may also be the result of an interaction between perfectly normal biology and a hostile socio-cultural environment.

Chapter 8
Human Nature and Deviance

> 'Tis evident that all the sciences have a
> relation, greater or less, to human nature;
> and that however wide any of them may seem
> to run from it, they will return back by one
> passage or another.
>
> David Hume, *A Treatise on Human Nature*

The social sciences have run very wide indeed but
there are intimations here and there that the "return
back" has begun. As is so often the case, the lead
has been taken by non-anthropologists. For example,
a distinguished brain researcher, Roger Sperry,
noting the earlier dominant view that the brain is
a blank slate, written upon almost entirely by experience, has said:

> Much of the basic scientific thinking and
> evidence behind this view has since suffered
> a series of severe upsets, leading to a cur-
> rent stand that is almost diametrically
> opposed to the earlier doctrines. Instead
> of a loose, universal plasticity in brain
> hookups, we now see a basic built-in wiring
> diagram, characteristic of the species and
> functionally rather rigid. (1965, p. 90)

Recently, Laughlin and D'Aquili (1974) have combined
neurological and anthropological perspectives in
their conclusion that man has inherited latent neural

structures that, like Jung's archetypes, provide genetically programmed models which determine the nature of human cognition.

The "road back" in the social sciences and humanities is still studded with obstacles, however. Many social scientists prefer Ortega y Gasset's famous dictum that "man has no nature; what he has is history." Views of anthropologists who are proponents of this notion of human plasticity such as Ashley Montagu (1956, 1968) or Clifford Geertz (1965) can be contrasted with views of those who advocate human nature, such as Anthony Wallace (1967) or Ernest Becker (1969). Unfortunately, debate in this area has often been confused by arguments concerning the uniqueness of human nature vis-à-vis animal nature. Such arguments typically focus on symbolic creativity or culture and neglect other aspects of human and animal nature (Spiro, 1954). These discussions have sometimes taken on political overtones, with scientists who are political conservatives espousing hereditarian ideas and liberal scientists preferring environmental views (Pastore, 1949). The difficulties involved in studying human nature are considerable and the dangers of error are great, yet the need to do so is greater still, for at the present time behavioral scientists make *implicit* assumptions about man's nature. If we hope to improve our understanding of human behavior, these assumptions about man's nature (including the assumption that he has none) must be set forth and examined (Goldschmidt, 1966).

We must begin by asking what is meant by human nature? As you might imagine, the difficulties begin here. As various students of deviant behavior have pointed out, no one has yet developed a theory of human nature that has received more than scattered or fleeting support. Even the meaning of the concept has been difficult to agree upon. Nevertheless, certain features of the concept can be specified. Human nature refers to man's biological inheritance. The concept assumes that some aspects of this

inheritance are sufficiently basic to man that they
will be expressed in all men, in all places. Culture
may modify man's inherent nature, even suppress it
almost totally, but it cannot obliterate it altogether.
It is also understood that not all aspects of human
nature are manifested early in life, so man's nature
may vary with age, perhaps even with sex, and, of
course, it will manifest itself variously depending
upon the intrauterine and life experiences of any
particular human. The concept is complex and difficult, but most basically it means man's shared,
inborn predisposition to respond to an environment
within certain limits. It is to the *presence*, not
absence, of such limits in man that the concept calls
our attention.

Given the difficulties of the concept itself,
how does one study human nature? If it exists, how
can it be discovered? While no method is without
difficulties (or we would have long since known all
there is to know about man), there are five general
procedures that have some demonstrable promise for
the study of human nature. First, the workings of
the human body itself can be examined. Here one
might be concerned with the effect of sex hormones,
or with the operation of the central nervous system.
We have already heard from Sperry with regard to
the brain, and we shall shortly consider a specific
localized brain function relevant to deviant behavior. All these matters can be considered in an
evolutionary perspective, as Hallowell (1960) has
done.

Second, one might experiment with humans to
ascertain the limits of their ability to behave in
certain ways. Our ability to experiment with humans
is curtailed by obvious moral considerations. It is
also limited by the serious problems of cross-cultural psychological testing. Nevertheless, such
experiments may have value, and we shall discuss
some relevant findings with respect to cognitive
dissonance and deviant behavior later. We might
also note that experiments have the potential for

discovering hitherto unsuspected attributes of man, attributes that no existing social or cultural environment has yet explored. For example, until Premack (1971) and others experimented with the ability of chimpanzees to deal with language, no one had known the extent of their capacity to live in a world of symbolic meaning. Indeed, Kroeber's (1928, p. 330) famous statement, "animals do not speak because they have nothing to say," was widely endorsed before Premack's work (Spiro, 1954).

Third, we can observe and experiment with infants in the first few days of life before their supposed "blank slates" have been very much written upon. One is limited here by the sensory-motor abilities of infants, but as the work of such investigators as Lewis Lipsitt shows, experiments with infants have substantial relevance to the study of human nature. Fourth, we may attempt to observe man everywhere, filtering out cultural differences in a search for human universals. Such a task is exceedingly difficult, as the few serious studies of universals have shown. Nevertheless, even here are important clues to man's nature and deviance, as the work of Ralph Linton suggests. Further, as Spiro (1954) has suggested, the fact that anthropologists (and others) have been able to visit different cultures all over the world and share the language and cultural reality of these people is strong intuitive support for the idea of a common human nature.

The final approach, and at the moment probably the most popular one, is to infer human nature primate behavior (Callan, 1970; Tiger and Fox, 1971). The findings of some of these investigators, such as Hans Kummer and Sherwood Washburn, may well be important for an understanding of human deviance. A recent book by Robert Hinde, *Biological Bases of Human Social Behaviour* (1974) illustrates this type of approach.

Whatever the method—and introspection seems to have been the most common one thus far—virtually every man of letters has left us some record

of his views on human nature. We have the contrasting views of Marx (man is totally determined by his
environment) and Sartre (man is totally free), as
well as those put forth by Plato, Skinner, and
Christianity (Stevenson, 1974). We also find that
there are differing views of human nature in India
and Greece, Israel and China, and in the Islamic and
Western worlds (Radhakrishnan and Raju, 1972). Men
in pre-literate societies also have their ideas about
human nature. As you might expect, those views most
often tell us about culture rather than man's nature.
      Where one begins a "scientific" study of human
nature is quite arbitrary. Some would insist that
it has yet to begin; others would refer to Pareto,
Weber, Mannheim, or Znaniecki. Most would agree
that Freud and Simmel were at least precursors; both
men emphasized man's natural aggressivity, finding
their evidence in the ease and pleasure with which
aggression or hostility is learned (recently, several writers have pointed to the evolutionary
necessity that organisms find it both easy and
pleasurable to learn what they must learn to survive).
One of the best known "theories" of human nature by
a social scientist is that of the sociologist, W. I.
Thomas, who postulated four universal "wishes" of
man: new experience, mastery or power, security, and
recognition by others. Others object that this list
is simply a culture-bound inference from experience
with Western man (Benthall, 1973).
      Perhaps the best-known modern anthropological
assay of human nature was by Malinowski (1944).
Unfortunately, Malinowski confined his study of
human nature to the basic physiological level of
metabolism, reproduction, health, etc. He then
derived universal cultural features from these, such
as, for example, "commissariat" from metabolism,
"kinship" from reproduction, and "hygiene" from
health. His *theory* convinced many readers that if
these common-sensical and somewhat simplistic formulations were the most that could be said about
human nature, then the entire subject was best left

alone   (Piddington, 1957). More favorable reaction
has been accorded the Freudian orientation of anthropologists such as Kluckhohn (1953), LeBarre (1954)
or Spiro (1954); the research of Piaget, Jung, or
Levi-Strauss on inborn logical operations of the
human mind (Laughlin and D'Aquili, 1974); the work
on the innate properties of the human mind with
regard to language (Lenneberg, 1967; Chomsky, 1968);
and the work of many ethologists and primatologists
from Lorenz' (1966) concern with aggression to Tiger
and Fox's effort to unravel the human "biogrammar"
(1971).

It may also repay us to examine the conclusions
of earlier anthropologists whose search for human
universals led them to think about *human nature*. For
example, Linton has argued for the crucial role of
boredom in human behavior. Linton felt that man's
continual elaboration of culture was as significant
as it was sometimes irrational. Since he could see
no necessary adaptive reason for this expansion of
cultural forms, he sought an *inner drive* and found
it in boredom. He noted that man everywhere seemed
to enjoy playing with his mind and his muscles for
no practical purpose. He attributed this capacity
to man's efforts to escape boredom. For Linton,
then, boredom was a critical feature of human nature,
and it lay "at the root of man's cultural advance"
(1936, p. 90). Later I shall suggest that boredom
may also play a part in man's deviant behavior.

Although it is still unusual for a social
scientist to provide a formal statement of his
theory of human nature, there are a few exceptions,
one of the most notable being sociologist Amitai
Etzioni in *The Active Society* (1968). Referring to
human needs and distinguishing these from "the
physiological ones that are common to man and animal,"
Etzioni posits the following six needs (1968, pp.
624-625): "(1) affection, (2) recognition (approval
by others), (3) context (orientation, meaning, whole-
ness, etc.), (4) repeated gratification, (5) stability
in the pattern of the distribution of rewards, and,

(6) variance in a social structure (a variety of
social roles and norms to provide outlets for human
individuality)." Etzioni's list may or may not
stand up to empirical scrutiny (his array of attributes probably is *not* confined to humans); it may
well presage a change in perspective in the social
sciences from an emphasis on tabula rasa and cultural relativism to one that includes basic human
nature, in terms of which social and cultural
adequacy can be measured.

Let me now attempt to illustrate how specific
information on human nature can be brought to bear
on the question of deviance. For this purpose I
shall consider only two aspects of human nature:
the (so-called) *flight/fight* mechanism, and what I
shall refer to as the *need for contrast*. That man
seeks to defend himself against threat is one of the
oldest truisms on record, but it should not be
ignored simply because it is well-recognized. Man
shares with other animals limbic brain mechanisms
that process information about threat, thereby per-
mitting the threatened animal (or person) to flee
or to fight as the situation requires. Mark and
Ervin (1970, p. 1) put it this way, rejecting as
they do so the idea that "violence" as such is an
aspect of human nature:

> Human beings do have instincts, but unprovoked
> violence is not among them. Instead, the in-
> stinct possessed by humans and represented by
> basic mechanisms in the central part of their
> brain is the instinct for *self-preservation*.
> And in threatening situations, this is trans-
> lated by a given individual into either flight
> or fight—more often the former than the latter.

Given the presence of this basic neural mechanism,
humans can very easily learn to be either timid or
aggressive.

There is experimental evidence suggesting the
presence of such a mechanism in infants as early as
the fourth day of life (Lipsitt, 1971). Lipsitt

reports that if a hand, blanket, or even a piece of
gauze is placed over the nose and mouth of an infant,
the result is a fixed sequence of behavior, an
unconditioned reflex or *instinct*. The following
sequence of actions takes place: (1) the infant's
head moves from side to side, (2) its head moves
backward, (3) its hands move to brush the obstruction
away, (4) its face reddens in vasodilation, (5) its
arms thrash about its face, and (6) it cries. We see
that an infant threatened by what Lipsitt has called
respiratory occlusion will first attempt to escape
from the noxious stimulation, only later producing
behavior that can be interpreted as "attack;" we
infer that the capacity for both behaviors exists
even in newborn infants.

In a search for security against similar threats,
man learns various strategies of flight and attack.
Perhaps a search for security lies behind the regular
primate pattern of dominance, closed groups, and
discrimination against outsiders (Kummer, 1971). Man
often establishes similar patterns but also learns to
recognize new threats in the symbolic world of his
own culture. Threats exist not only to life, but to
self-esteem, and both threats must be avoided, for
humans live not only in fear of death, but of dis-
grace as well. Consequently, people seek to predict
and to control their environments in order to reduce
the probability of threat just as they learn to
avoid or overcome threats once they occur. With a
flight-fight mechanism built into the human brain,
and with the human world of symbols creating new
threats with each day of life, it is little wonder
that people so often commit troublesome rule violations in pursuit of their self-interest, security, or
survival. Humans often learn to seek security
through cooperation and selflessness, but they are
just as often—perhaps always—vulnerable to selfish-
ness. The Ik of Uganda, with their single-minded
determination to survive no matter what the cost to
other Ik, are a catastrophic case in point (Turnbull,
1972). It is not just the Ik, however; humans every-

where have been recorded as violating the rules of
their societies by unfairly improving their own
position (and security) at the expense of their
fellow men.   Violence is only one means man may
learn to employ in his search for security.   Love
(and through it, trust) is another (Stayton *et al.*,
1971).   Given the human flight-fight mechanism, the
potential always exists that people may individualize
their survival, and even become deviant by pursuing
their own self-interest at the expense of others.

    Although details of the relationship between a
flight-fight mechanism and human deviance remain
speculative, the position I have developed here
will probably be accepted by many, at least in its
general outline.   Let us turn now to another possible relationship, this time one which is highly
speculative.   It is offered here as an example of
how one might think about the linkage of *human
nature*—in this case boredom—and *deviance*.

    We have already encountered Linton's idea that
man's intolerance for boredom is at the heart of
his cultural elaborations.   Freud (1930) noted that
man seems to be the sort of creature who can experience intense pleasure only through contrast.   In
these two comments an important attribute of human
nature is suggested, namely, that man has a need
for contrast or variety.   There is some experimental
evidence in support of this idea.   For example,
human preference for variation has been reported
in all sensory modalities from food, color, and
sound, to sex, and even two-day-old infants prefer
alternation in the taste of their food to sameness
(Lipsitt, 1971).   It is also known that the extreme
absence of contrast, as in sensory deprivation, will
not simply bore but can disable or even kill a human.
While it is true that man will seek to avoid or
resolve ambiguity and cognitive dissonance, it is
also the case that man will tolerate and even actively seek some ambiguity and some dissonance (Abelson
et al., 1968).   There is also a sizable psychological literature which reports that humans seek variety

(Berlyne, 1960; Fiske and Maddi, 1961). It has
been reported (London, Schubert and Washburn, 1972),
that while sensory deprivation decreases cortical
arousal (EEG), psychological boredom increases autonomic arousal (GSR, skin conductance and heart rate),
thus preparing humans to seek increased levels of
activity and variety. Ethologists such as Eibl-
Eibesfeldt (1970) have also concluded that human
curiosity and search for new experience are inborn
drives which we share with animals. The neurochem-
ical source of a need for contrast is not known, but
we might speculate that man everywhere lives in a
world where information is fundamentally defined as
a "bit," or a "difference that makes a difference"
as Bateson has said (1972). Perhaps our nervous
systems are built not only to perceive contrast but
to seek meaning in it.

     Should a need for contrast exist as an attribute
of human nature, its significance for deviance lies
in the possibility that once a primary need for
security has been established in a predictable and
stable environment, people will tend to become *bored*
and may seek new experiences or variety even though
such contrasts involve danger or risk of rule violation ("adventure" or "change of pace" are terms we
often use). Societies with elastic rules may successfully permit contrast-seeking behavior within
the limits of what is permissible; more confining
societies may compel people to deviate in order to
satisfy their need for contrast. In this latter
type of society, people will be forced to balance
their need for security against their boredom.
People may abandon secure (but boring) ways for more
dangerous variety; when they do, trouble can easily
result, with people then seeking security anew. This
dialectic or alternation may be an aspect of what has
so often been seen as man's dual nature, his *beast*
and his *angel* in Aristotle's terms, or his *Yin* and
Yang for the Chinese.

     We should also note the possibility that human
nature may vary significantly between men and women,

and that these differences may provide yet another
set of possibilities for deviance. Such differences
have been discussed by Tiger (1969) and Tiger and Fox
(1971); the response to their views has been heated
and polemical. Their position may be summarized as
follows: since 99% of human evolution was spent in
societies that survived by hunting and gathering,
and since men and women probably had quite different
roles to play in such societies (men finding and
killing game, women tending the children and gathering near the safety of camp), it is possible that
men and women have evolved somewhat different biologically based abilities, needs and predispositions
(Washburn and Lancaster, 1968; Brown, 1970). Evidence
is equivocal thus far but there is reason to believe
that males are more likely than females to be aggressive and exploratory. These differences are also
found among non-human primates, so hunting and gathering evolution may not be the causal factor involved
(Kummer, 1971). Other possible differences include
greater spatio-temporal ability for males and greater
verbal ability for females as well as a tendency for
males to orient visually while females orient in an
aural-oral modality. Male-female antagonism and
conflict is surely a product of history and of culture, but it may also be rooted in the kinds of
biological differences discussed above. If it is,
then deviance may have still another biological
source.
     Despite centuries of speculation, far too little
is known about human nature to permit us to say much
more than we have. The concept may in fact be so
simple as to be misleading, for humans assuredly
have no *single* nature, but several, and these natures
may have built-in tensions, oppositions and conflicts.
Furthermore, just as men and women may differ in their
natures, so may the young and the old, and individual
differences must always be reckoned with. Whatever
the future holds with respect to the concept of human
nature, it is obvious that human biology and human
behavior *are* related and, therefore, deviant behavior

must also have some biological foundation. The study of human nature is important because it calls attention to the ways in which human biology may contribute to deviance *as well as* conformity. As we have seen, explanations of deviance are based on assumptions about human nature. Without an explicit theory of human nature, these assumptions will continue to be implicit, and because implicit theories are not brought into the open, they explain little, while they confound a great deal. Although *human nature* has often been declared disreputable and defunct, this hydra-headed concept has inevitably returned to bedevil those who would attempt to understand man without explicit reference to it.

Chapter 9

The Nature of Society

An understanding of deviant behavior requires not only that we explore the intricacies of human nature, but also that we inquire into the nature of the societies in which humans live. What are societies really like? They differ, needless to say, with some tending toward the strict regulations of commandos on military duty and others approximating the casual understandings that guide good friends on a Sunday picnic. Beyond such obviously extreme cases there remains the question of how we as social scientists conceptualize human society. There are two competing models of society, one traditional, the other challenging for acceptance. The conventional model can be called "equilibrium," the other "tension management" (Moore, 1963).

The equilibrium model of society has enjoyed virtually unchallenged dominance in the social sciences until quite recently. In brief, this model is based on the theory of functionalism and has found eloquent spokesmen in such important figures as Talcott Parsons and A. R. Radcliffe-Brown. Equilibrium is based on the assumption that man is highly malleable, and is consequently easily and fully socialized. Given such fully socialized men, the society achieves equilibrium and all change in the system must emanate from the outside (from class conflict, from alien cultures, or from natural calamities). When change

occurs, the society self-corrects toward balance.
As a result, change is meaningless or destructive,
for it is either neutralized or it tears the system
apart. The equilibrium model assumes that social
order is the natural outcome of human existence.
This is the conventional theory that underlies the
folk-urban comparison.

The tension management model is a recent con-
testant for widespread acceptance into the social
sciences. It does not assume man to be fully malleable, assuming instead that man is *never* fully
socialized. In such a social order, change is
intrinsic as well as extrinsic. Furthermore, the
reaction to change, from whatever source, may either
reduce or produce tension. Society is, therefore,
not seen as being in balance, and its response to
change is not necessarily toward restoring balance.
Just as change can be destructive, it can also be
important and positive, leading to new social and
cultural forms. In this view, human existence creates
tension which must somehow be managed. Social order
is difficult to achieve, and any period of social
stability is to be regarded as an accomplishment
(Moore, 1963; Etzioni, 1968; Murphy, 1972).

Which model best fits the facts about deviant
behavior in folk societies? Before attempting to
provide an answer we must discuss three considerations: (1) the sources of variability in a socio-
cultural system, (2) the nature of cultural rules,
and (3) the nature of social control mechanisms.
Sources of variability exist in any society, however
small or simple it may be. In addition to the
presence of significant temperamental individuality
as discussed earlier, every human society contains
variability as the result of differences in age, sex,
kin relationships (father, child, uncle, sister, etc.),
physical abilities (strength, size, endurance, agil-
ity, visual acuity, etc.), and intellectual abilities
(memory, problem-solving, semantic capacity, percep-
tual skill, etc.). In addition, such individual
differences can be exaggerated by socialization

practices which inevitably differ somewhat from family to family, as well as by idiosyncratic experiences that affect certain individuals and not others.
All these factors are present in every human society.
In addition, most societies add variability based on
economic or religious specialization, as well as
status or class differentiations that involve wealth,
power, or prestige. Every society must accommodate
itself to various differences among its members.
Given this universal fact of variability, we must
ask ourselves what kinds of rules societies have
developed, and how these rules are maintained or
enforced.

We have seen that people throughout the world
sometimes violate the rules of their societies and
consequently find themselves in trouble. We must
now ask about the nature of rules that human beings
make, generally follow, and sometimes break. Are
these rules so clear-cut and simple that they are
understood by all? Or are they complicated, unclear
and given to frequent misinterpretation? To answer
these questions we must first realize that the term
"rule" can refer to various kinds of understandings
among people (Gibbs, 1965). It could refer to an
expectation between two lovers that they will give
up smoking, to a standard of etiquette concerning
how full a wine glass should be poured, to a common understanding about how one greets a friend, or
to a law about stealing. Some of these rules affect
only two people; others affect all members of a society. Some, like filling wine glasses, are poorly
understood by most people; others, like saying hello
to a friend, are widely known and accepted. Some,
like stealing, can bring serious trouble if violated;
others, like failing to go to church on Sunday can
have various consequences—a serious offense for some
and no offense at all for others.

Some rules are so deeply internalized that they
are obeyed unconsciously. Thus we speak, sit, walk,
ride in an elevator, or make love according to rules
about which we are relatively unaware. If asked, we

might be able to specify the rules for riding in an
elevator but we could not specify all the rules that
govern our speaking, especially the grammatical ones.
Other rules are conscious and may not be internalized
at all. Laws, especially those we dislike, are like
this. For example, most college students in this
country would probably be able to specify the law
regarding marijuana, but many who obey the law do
so not because they have internalized it, but because
it is enforced by severe penalties. People everywhere regulate their behavior in terms of many shared
understandings, conscious or unconscious, about what
is expected, proper, lawful, reasonable and the like.

A. K. Cohen (1966, pp. 3-4) has summarized matters well:

> Whatever we may think of Hobbes' argument, he
> saw one thing clearly: if human beings are to
> do business with one another, there must be
> rules, and people must be able to assume that,
> by and large, these rules will be observed . . .
> Of course, it does not follow that the rules
> must provide a blueprint for every human gesture.
> There is always some room, and often the neces-
> sity, for the exercise of discretion or inclina-
> tion. Every system can tolerate a certain amount
> of ambiguity, uncertainty, and even confusion,
> and there are no doubt many rules that regulate
> conduct with such precision and detail that they
> thwart rather than facilitate the accomplishment
> of human purposes.

Cohen gives us the answer to our original question: some rules are clear and unequivocal, but many
others are not. It is important in the study of
deviance to note that many rules are not clear or
simple but are instead complex, contradictory and
ambiguous. We have already seen in Meggitt's account
of the Walbiri of Australia that some rules can
simply be too complicated for everyone to follow.
How people construe, maintain and respond to such
complexity has been well-described and analyzed by

sociologists influenced by Wittgenstein, Schutz and
Garfinkel (McHugh, 1968; Garfinkel, 1967; Sudnow,
1972). Some rules are not merely complex, they are
contradictory as well. Perhaps as a consequence,
most societies have rules about how to break rules
as well as rules about what to do after the rule
has been broken. Presumably such contingency rules
are necessary because, in part at least, by following one rule one sometimes breaks another (Keesing,
1967).

In addition to being complex and contradictory,
some rules are highly ambiguous. It could be argued,
as Wittgenstein has done, that all rules have elements
of ambiguity but some rules are plainly more ambiguous
than others. In our own society, for example, the
rule (law) which states that automobiles must drive
to the right is reasonably unambiguous. There are
exceptions such as passing to the left, avoiding
children who run into the street, or obeying a
police order, but generally people know the rule
and follow it—largely, one presumes, as a matter of
survival since error could be costly. Lest we
assume that all aspects of human life which are extremely dangerous are regulated by unambiguous rules,
it would be well to consider a recent case of TWA
Flight 514 which crashed on its approach to Wash-
ington, D. C., December 1, 1974, killing all 92
persons aboard. One would think that matters as
important as getting large airliners up in the air
and back down again safely would be serious enough
for anyone, and that rules of air-traffic control
(which regulate takeoff and landing) and pilot compliance would be precisely worked out. As this case
so tragically demonstrated, nothing could be less
true. In addition to the fact that a mountain in the
path of the descending aircraft was not properly
charted (for the pilot or the controller) subsequent
testimony brought out the alarming point that pilots
often use one set of manuals and regulations while
controllers use another. Also, pilots and controllers

employ differing terminologies, their interpretations of the rules openly conflict, and confusion is commonplace (*Los Angeles Times*. February 1, 1975).

Marvin Harris (1970, p. 12) has argued that some ambiguity, such as that involving how Brazilians sort one another into racial categories concerning greater or lesser amounts of African blood, may be functional by maintaining noise and disagreement (and hence avoiding class and caste distinctions which would be incompatible with Brazilian society and ideology). Heinz Hohne (1971) has reported that the rules by which the Nazi SS operated before and during World War II were intentionally ambiguous in order to give their leaders room to indulge their wills. Why the rules regulating air traffic should sometimes be ambiguous is more difficult to say.

It is also important to note that when rules are complex, contradictory and ambiguous they lend themselves to argument, manipulation and negotiation. Excellent examples of the manipulability of rules in non-Western societies are provided by Goldschmidt (1969), Bailey (1969), and many others. It is impossible to generalize about rules in all societies without some distortion, but a conclusion that seems to summarize the nature of most rules in most societies is this: rules are so constituted that at least some people can manipulate them to their advantage. Anthropologist W. E. H. Stanner (1959, p. 216) reached a conclusion with regard to an African society that can stand, in my opinion, for all societies:

> It can be argued sensibly that it is precisely
> . . .the manipulative, bargaining, transactional
> approach to life, which *is* the system of their
> life. In other words . . .'endemic conflict'
> (including 'exceptions' to the 'rules') is not
> an upset or defect or an aberration or a fiction
> of some idealized or perfect system, but is
> *itself* the system, together with the accompani-
> ments and consequences which, logically, follow

when most interests can be attained only through other people, i.e., on terms either of agreement or of force.

Given man's variability and the elasticity of his rules, means of social control are obviously necessary. All societies attempt to control their members without force, as equilibrium theory has it, by socializing them so that they want to behave as they must behave. Control by socialization may utilize reward, fear, shame, guilt, and the like, and it can be extremely effective, depending on the internalization of values and the desire for approval by others. For example, the Mixtec Indians of the town of Juxtlahuaca, Oaxaca, Mexico, whose almost total absence of violence we discussed earlier, have developed a powerful technique for teaching children to avoid violence. They teach children that the feeling of anger will, if not quickly overcome, lead them to illness and possibly death. This belief serves to inhibit not only the expression of overt aggression—which would be disruptive to life in the barrio— but angry thoughts as well (Romney and Romney, 1963). Another strategy was employed by the Sioux Indians (Erikson, 1950), who used visions to channel individuals into or away from deviant roles. Young Sioux sought visions which would guide them in the course of their adult lives. These visions, or dreams, were reported to adults for interpretation and as a result a young person might be labeled a great warrior, fine hunter, creative artist, shaman— or a deviant. Some visions traditionally led to the label of clown, homosexual or prostitute. Presumably these visions, the content of which was widely known, reflected an individual's long-standing, even unconscious, fears or wishes rather than merely being random, whimsical or accidental. Such visions may have served to offer an acceptable escape from the demands of ordinary life (as a warrior or wife) into a more deviant, but compatible role, based as Erikson notes, not on the individual's personal decision, but

on supernatural intervention instead. Such deviants
then were permitted to play a secondary role among
the Sioux, not a totally degraded nor rejected one,
and the potential for trouble was greatly reduced.
    Internal techniques of social control such as
these are said to be successful because, as Locke
or modern functionalists would have it, people
recognize that there is an advantage in maintaining
their associations with one another and so they continue their reciprocities and exchanges and they
uphold custom. No society has been able to exist,
however, without recourse to external controls as
well. Therefore, societies also employ gossip,
witchcraft, ridicule, fines, and various threats of
physical coercion. Sometimes, as is typical in *folk*
societies, these external controls are mild, involving jokes, persuasion, ritual or temporary ostracism.
These folk societies may also control their members'
behavior through religious belief or by means of
witchcraft. In such societies, people may avoid
breaking rules and giving offense to one another
primarily to escape supernatural retribution or,
more commonly, retaliatory witchcraft. More serious
deviance may be avoided because people are fearful
of beginning a quarrel that could escalate into a
feud leading to continuing bloodshed between clans.
Here the fear is not merely one of individual antagonism but of collective and continuing conflict. So
ubiquitous and powerful are the constraining influences of fear of witchcraft and feud in many folk
societies that anthropologist Elizabeth Colson (1974,
p. 45) has concluded:

> Fear, to most of us, seems a poor basis on which
> to found a society or develop a system of law.
> But we are unrealistic if we ignore the fear
> and concentrate solely on the advantages people
> see in their associations.

Other societies, especially those that have moved
away from "folkness" toward more urban forms of gov-
ernance, have relied on law, police powers and court

systems to control the behavior of their members. **We**
must conclude that some people follow rules primarily
due to external constraints. Were this not so, it
would be difficult to understand why such constraints
should be present in all societies.

Social systems, which seem to mirror man's nature
and his diversity, are characterized by variability,
complexity, ambiguity, and trouble. Durkheim was
right in saying that rules themselves create the possibility of deviance, but it is also true that men
create rules that permit them to maneuver to their
advantage and to behave within one rule while violating another.

It would appear that equilibrium theory is an
inadequate model upon which to base one's understanding of folk society. The tension-management model
better fits the facts of man's behavior and his social
and cultural arrangements in societies throughout the
world. The major implication of this conclusion for
the study of deviance is this: man is not fully
malleable and in his recalcitrance toward complete
sociability he possesses the potential for causing
trouble. Viable social systems must be able to cope
with this potential.

Conclusion

Our present cross-cultural knowledge of deviance, like
our knowledge of many things, is not all that we would
like it to be. As with most other things, the passage
of time will no doubt improve our understanding, but
there are some problems concerning the study of
deviance that have complicated our research in the
past and are likely to continue to do so in the
future. Deviance includes such a diversity of phenomena that one hardly knows where to begin. Perhaps
for this reason, anthropology has tended to isolate
the study of *deviants* from the study of *deviance*.
Deviants—deviant persons or marginal men—have been a
focus for study in what is now called psychological
anthropology (formerly called culture and personality),
while the study of deviance—of rule violation as such—
has been dealt with separately, usually by anthropologists concerned with law, social control or social
organization. Today, many anthropologists continue
to think of the study of deviance primarily in terms
of deviant persons, not deviant acts.

    This division of study, while understandable in
light of anthropology's history of specialization,
has been a barrier to understanding. It should now
be clear that the study of deviance must include both
deviant acts and deviant persons. We need to know
why some men become deviants, while others—who also
break rules—do not. We need to know why men break

rules in the first place, and why only *some* rules,
some times, and why the consequences of rule violation
are so variable. We also need to know why societies
differ in the kind, frequency, and seriousness of
deviance, and what purpose is served by labeling some
of their members as deviants.

If we are to improve our understanding so that
we can begin to answer these questions, we must enlarge
our study to include everything having to do with misbehavior. Many social scientists have reached this
same conclusion, but in doing so they have also come
upon a sobering realization. To study misbehavior,
one must also study proper behavior. To learn why
men sometimes misbehave, one must also learn why they
so often behave as they should. This realization
is sobering for it forces us to study deviance as
only one among many aspects of man-in-society. And
so deviance becomes not simpler to deal with, but
very much more complicated.

This reformulation is challenging, but it is
nevertheless necessary. This is so because *all* people
misbehave. We will never better our understanding
of human misbehavior until we better our theories of
human nature, and of the social and cultural worlds
in which humans live. What is more, not only will
we fail to improve our understanding of deviance
until we integrate its study into a general theory
of man-in-society, but our understanding of man-in-
society will also be inadequate.

References

Abelson, R. P., *et al.*, *Theories of Cognitive Consistency*. Chicago: Rand McNally, 1968.

Ammar, H., *Growing up in an Egyptian Village*. London: Routledge and Kegan Paul, 1954.

Arensberg, C., *The Irish Countryman*. Gloucester, Mass.: Peter Smith, 1959.

Ashley Montagu, M. F., *The Biosocial Nature of Man*. New York: Grove Press, 1956.

_____*Man and Aggression*. New York: Oxford University Press, 1968.

Austin, J. L., *Philosophical Papers*. London: Oxford University Press, 1968.

Bailey, F. G., *Strategems and Spoils: A Social Anthropology of Politics*. Oxford: Blackwell, 1969.

Bandura, A., and Walters, R. H., *Social Learning and Personality Development*. New York: Holt, Rinehart and Winston, 1963.

Baroja, J. C., The City and the Country: Reflexions on Some Ancient Commonplaces. In J. Pitt-Rivers (ed.), *Mediterranean Countrymen*. Paris: Moulton, 1963, pp. 27-40.

Bateson, G., *Steps to an Ecology of Mind*. San Francisco: Chandler, 1972.

Beals, A., *Culture in Process*. New York: Holt, Rinehart and Winston, 1967.

Becker, E., *Angel in Armor: A Post-Freudian Perspective on the Nature of Man*. New York: The Free Press, 1969.

113

Belo, J., The Balinese Temper. *Character and Personality*. 4: 120-146, 1935.

Benedict, R., *Patterns of Culture*. Boston: Houghton Mifflin, 1934.

Bennett, J. W., The Interpretation of Pueblo Culture: A Question of Values. In D. G. Haring (ed.), *Personal Character and Cultural Milieu*. Syracuse, New York: Syracuse University Press, 1956.

Benthall, J. (ed.), *The Limits of Human Nature*. New York: E. P. Dutton, 1974.

Berlyne, D. E., *Conflict, Arousal, and Curiosity*. New York: McGraw-Hill, 1960.

Birch, H. G., and Gussow, J. D., *Disadvantaged Children: Health, Nutrition and School Failure*. New York: Harcourt, Brace and World, 1970.

Bloch, M., (translated by L. Nanyon), *Feudal Society*. London: Routledge and Kegan Paul, 1961.

Blum, A., and McHugh, P., The Social Ascription of Motives. *American Sociological Review*. 36: 98-109, 1971.

Blum, R., *Society and Drugs*, Vol. I. San Francisco: Jossey-Bass, 1969.

Blythe, R., *Akenfield: Portrait of an English Village*. New York: Delta, 1969.

Bohannan, P. (ed.), *African Homicide and Suicide*. Princeton: Princeton University Press, 1960.

Bowen, E. S., *Return to Laughter*. New York: Doubleday, 1964.

Briggs, J. L., *Never in Anger: Portrait of an Eskimo Family*. Cambridge, Massachusetts: Harvard University Press, 1970.

Brown, J. K., A Note on the Division of Labor by Sex. *American Anthropologist*. 72: 1073-1078, 1970.

Bruner, E. M., Urbanization and Ethnic Identity in North Sumatra. *American Anthropologist*. 63: 508-521, 1961.

Burrow, E. G., and Spiro, M. E., *An Atoll Culture: Ethnography of Ifaluk in the Central Carolines*. New Haven: Human Relations Area Files, 1953.

Callan, H., *Ethology and Society: Towards an Anthropological View*. Oxford: Clarendon Press, 1970.

Carstairs, G., Daru and Bhang: Cultural Factors in the Choice of Intoxicant. *Quart. J. Studies on Alcohol*. 15: 220-237, 1954.

Castaneda, C., *The Teachings of Don Juan*. Berkeley: University of California Press, 1968.

_____ *A Separate Reality*. New York: Simon and Schuster, 1971.

Chagnon, N. A., *Yanomamö: The Fierce People*. New York: Holt, Rinehart and Winston, 1968.

Chapple, E., *Culture and Biological Man*. New York: Holt, Rinehart and Winston, 1970.

Chomsky, N., *Language and Mind*. New York: Harcourt, Brace and World, 1968.

Cloward, R. A., and Ohlin, L. B., *Delinquency and Opportunity: A Theory of Delinquent Gangs*. Glencoe, Ill.: The Free Press, 1960.

Cohen, A. K., *Deviance and Control*. Englewood Cliffs, New Jersey: Prentice-Hall, 1966.

Cohen, Y., *The Transition from Childhood to Adolescence*. Chicago: Aldine, 1964.

Colson, E., *Tradition and Contract: The Problem of Order*. Chicago: Aldine, 1974.

Cravioto, J., Nutritional Deficiencies and Mental Performance in Childhood. In D. C. Glass (ed.), *Environmental Influences*. New York: The Rockefeller University Press, 1968, pp. 3-51.

Devereux, G., Mohave Ethnopsychiatry and Suicide: The Psychiatric Knowledge and Psychic Disturbances of an Indian Tribe. *Bureau of American Ethnology*, Bulletin 175, 1961.

DeVos, G., Suicide in Cross-Cultural Perspective. In H. Resnick (ed.), *Suicidal Behaviors*. New York: Little, Brown, 1968.

DiCara, L. V., Learning in the Autonomic Nervous System. *Scientific American*. 222: 30-39, 1970.

Dobkin de Rios, M., *Visionary Vine: Psychedelic Healing in the Peruvian Amazon*. San Francisco: Chandler, 1972.

Drum Magazine,   185: 5-8, 1966.
Durkheim, E., *Le Suicide: Étude de Sociologie.*
  Paris: Presses Universitaires de France, 1897.
_____   *The Rules of the Sociological Method.* New
  York: The Free Press, 1938.
Eccles, J. C., *The Understanding of the Brain.* New
  York: McGraw-Hill, 1973.
Edgerton, R. B., Pokot Intersexuality: An East
  African Example of Sexual Incongruity. *American
  Anthropologist.* 66: 1288-1299, 1964.
_____   On the "Recognition" of Mental Illness. In
  S. Plog and R. Edgerton (eds.), *Changing Perspec-
  tives in Mental Illness.* New York: Holt,
  Rinehart and Winston, 1969, pp. 49-72.
_____   Mental Retardation in Non-Western Societies:
  Toward a Cross-Cultural Perspective on Incompe-
  tence. In H. C. Haywood (ed.), *Social-Cultural
  Aspects of Mental Retardation.* New York: Apple-
  ton-Century-Crofts, 1970, pp. 523-559.
Edgerton, R. B., and Conant, F. P., Kilapat: The
  "Shaming Party" Among the Pokot of East Africa.
  Southwest J. Anthropology. 20: 404-418, 1964.
Eibl-Eibesfeldt, I., *Ethology.* New York: Holt,
  Rinehart and Winston, 1970.
Eisenstadt, S. N., *From Generation to Generation:
  Age Groups and Social Structure.* Glencoe, Illi-
  nois: The Free Press, 1956.
Embree, J., Thailand—A Loosely Structured Social
  System. *American Anthropologist.* 52: 181-193,
  1950.
Erikson, E., *Childhood and Society.* New York:
  Norton, 1950.
Erikson, K., *Wayward Puritans: A Study in the So-
  ciology of Deviance.* New York: Wiley, 1966.
Escalona, S. K., *The Roots of Individuality: Nor-
  mal Patterns of Development in Infancy.* Chicago:
  Aldine, 1968.
Etzioni, A., *The Active Society.* New York: Free
  Press, 1968.

Evans-Pritchard, E. E., Sexual Inversion Among the
Azande. *American Anthropologist.* 72: 1428-1433,
1970.

Fernandez, J. S., Bantu Brotherhood: Symmetry, Socialization, and Choice in Two Bantu Cultures.
Kinship and Culture. Chicago: Aldine, 1971,
pp. 339-366.

Firth, R., Suicide and Risk-Taking in Tikopia Society. *Psychiatry.* 24: 1-17, 1961.

Fiske, D. W., and Maddi, S. R., *Functions of Varied
Experience.* Homewood, Ill.: Dorsey Press, 1961.

Flannery, R., Individual Variation in Culture. In
A. F. C. Wallace (ed.), *Men and Cultures.* Phila-
delphia: University of Pennsylvania Press, 1960,
pp. 87-92.

Fortune, R. F., *Sorcerers of Dobu.* New York:
Morrow, 1932.

Freud, S., (trans. by Joan Riviere), *Civilization
and its Discontents.* London: L. and Virginia
Woolf at the Hogarth Press, 1930.

Friedl, E., *Vasilika: A Village in Modern Greece.*
New York: Holt, Rinehart and Winston, 1964.

Furst, P. T., *Flesh of the Gods: The Ritual Use of
Hallucinogens.* New York: Praeger, 1972.

Gardner, P., Symmetric Respect and Memorate Knowledge:
The Structure and Ecology of the Individualistic
Culture. *Southwestern J. Anthropology.* 22: 389-
415, 1966.

Garfinkel, H., *Studies in Ethnomethodology.* Englewood Cliffs, New Jersey: Prentice-Hall, 1967.

Geertz, C., The Impact of the Concept of Culture
on the Concept of Man. In J. Platt (ed.), *New
Views on Human Nature.* Chicago: University of
Chicago Press, 1965, pp. 93-118.

_____ *The Interpretation of Cultures.* New York:
Basic Books, 1973.

Gibbs, J. P., Norms: The Problem of Definition
and Classification. *American Journal of Sociology.* 70: 586-594, 1965.

Goldschmidt, W., *Comparative Functionalism. An Essay
in Anthropological Theory.* Berkeley: University
of California Press, 1966.

_____*Kambuya's Cattle: The Legacy of an African Herdsman.*   Berkeley: University of California Press, 1969.

Goodman, M. E., *The Individual and Culture.*   Homewood, Ill.:   Dorsey, 1967.

Gorer, G., *Himalayan Village: An Account of the Lepchas of Sikkim.*   London: Michael Joseph, 1938.

Gouldner, A., *The Coming Crisis of Western Sociology.*   New York: Basic Books, 1970.

Green, R., Homosexuality as a Mental Illness.   *International Journal of Psychiatry.*   10: 77-98, 1972.

_____*Sexual Identity Conflict in Children and Adults.*   New York: Basic Books, 1973.

Gusinde, M., *The Yamana.*   New Haven: Human Relations Area Files, 1961.

Hallowell, A. I., Self, Society and Culture in Phylogenetic Perspective.   In S. Tax (ed.), *Evolution after Darwin,* Vol. II.   Chicago: University of Chicago Press, 1960, pp. 309-371.

Harner, M. (ed.), *Hallucinogens and Shamanism.*   London: Oxford University Press, 1973.

Harris, G., Possession "Hysteria" in a Kenya Tribe.   *American Anthropologist.*   59: 1046-1066, 1957.

Harris, M., Referential Ambiguity in the Calculus of Brazilian Racial Identity.   *Southwestern Journal of Anthropology.*   26: 1-14, 1970.

Hart, C. W. M., The Sons of Turimpi.   *American Anthropologist.*   56: 242-261, 1954.

Hart, H. L. A., The Ascription of Responsibility and Rights.   In A. Flew (ed.), *Logic and Language.*   Oxford: Basil Blackwell, 1960, pp. 145-166.

Heath, D. B., Drinking Patterns of the Bolivian Camba.   *Quarterly J. of Studies on Alcohol.*   19: 491-508, 1958.

Henry, J., *Jungle People: A Kaingáng Tribe of the Highlands of Brazil.*   Richmond, Virginia: J. J. Augustin, 1941.

_____The Personal Community and its Invariant Properties.   *American Anthropologist.*   60: 827-831, 1958.

Hinde, R. A., *Biological Bases of Human Social Behavior.*   New York: McGraw-Hill, 1974.

Hippler, A. E., Fusion and Frustration: Dimensions in the Cross-Cultural Ethnopsychology of Suicide. *American Anthropologist.* 71: 1074-1087, 1969.

Hirschi, T., *Causes of Delinquency.* Berkeley: University of California Press, 1969.

Hohne, H., *The Order of the Death's Head: The Story of Hitler's SS.* New York: Ballantine, 1971.

Holmberg, A. R., *Nomads of the Long Bow.* New York: Natural History Press, 1969.

Kaplan, B. H., *Psychiatric Disorder and the Urban Environment.* New York: Behavioral Publications, 1971.

Katz, S. H., and Foulks, E. F., Mineral Metabolism and Behavior: Abnormalities of Calcium Homeostasis. *Amer. J. Physical Anthropology.* 32: 299-304, 1970.

Keesing, R., Statistical Models and Decision Models of Social Structure: A Kwaio Case. *Ethnology.* 4: 1-6, 1967.

Khalil, M. S., Suicidal Behavior in Cairo. *The National Review of Criminal Science.* 5: 14-20, 1962.

Kluckhohn, C.; Murray, H. A.; and Schneider, D. M., *Personality in Nature, Society and Culture.* 2nd ed., New York: A. A. Knopf, 1955.

Kroeber, A. L., Sub-Human Beginnings. *Quarterly Review of Biology,* 3: 325-42, 1928.

Kummer, H., *Primate Societies.* Chicago: Aldine, 1971.

LaBarre, W., *The Human Animal.* Chicago: University of Chicago Press, 1954.

Lamson, H. D., *Social Pathology in China.* Shanghai: Commercial Press, 1934.

Langness, L. L., *The Life History in Anthropological Science.* New York: Holt, Rinehart and Winston, 1965.

_____ Hysterical Psychosis in the New Guinea Highlands: A Bena Bena Example. *Psychiatry.* 28: 259-277, 1965a.

_____ Personal Communication, 1972.

Laslett, P., *The World We Have Lost: England Before the Industrial Age*. New York: Charles Scribner's Sons, 1965.

Laughlin, C. D., Jr., and D'Aquili, E. G., Biogenetic Structuralism. New York: Columbia University Press, 1974.

Leach, E., *Pul Eliya. A Village in Ceylon*. London: Cambridge University Press, 1961.

Lenneberg, E. H., *The Biological Foundation of Language*. New York: Wiley, 1967.

LeVine, R. A., Gusii Sex Offenses: A Study in Social Control. *American Anthropologist*. 61: 965-990, 1959.

Levi-Strauss, C., *A World on the Wane*. London: Hutchinson, 1961.

Lewis, O., *Life in a Mexican Village: Tepoztlan Restudied*. Urbana, Ill.: University of Illinois Press, 1951.

Lindblom, G., *The Akamba in British East Africa*, Volume 17 (2nd ed.). Uppsala: Archives D'Etudes Orientales, 1920.

Lindesmith, A. R., and Strauss, A. L., A Critique of Culture-Personality Writings. *American Sociological Review*. 15: 587-600, 1950.

Linton, R., *The Study of Man*. New York: Appleton-Century-Crofts, 1936.

Lipsitt, L. P., Infant Anger: Toward an Understanding of the Ontogenesis of Human Aggression. Paper delivered at UCLA Symposium on Biology and Behavior, March 4, 1971.

London, H.; Schubert, D. S.; and Washburn, D., Increase of Autonomic Arousal by Boredom. *Journal of Abnormal Psychology*. 80: 29-36, 1972.

Lorenz, K. Z., (translated by Marjorie Kerr Wilson), *On Aggression*. New York: Harcourt, Brace and World, 1966.

MacAndrew, C., and Edgerton, R. B., *Drunken Comportment: A Social Explanation*. Chicago: Aldine, 1969.

Madge, J., *The Origins of Scientific Sociology*. New York: The Free Press, 1962.

Malinowski, B., *Argonauts of the Western Pacific*. New York: E. P. Dutton, 1926.

_____ *A Scientific Theory of Culture*. Chapel Hill, N. C.: University of North Carolina Press, 1944.

Mangin, W. (ed.), *Peasants in Cities*. Boston: Houghton Mifflin Co., 1970.

Mark, V. H., and Ervin, F. R., *Violence and the Brain* New York: Harper & Row, 1970.

Marmor, J., *Modern Psychoanalysis. New Directions and Perspectives*. New York: Basic Books, 1968.

Matthieson, P., *Under the Mountain Wall*. New York: Ballantine, 1962.

Matza, D., *Becoming Deviant*. Englewood Cliffs, New Jersey: Prentice-Hall, 1969.

Maugh, T. H., Diabetes: Epidemiology Suggests a Viral Connection. *Science*. 188: 347-351, 1975.

McHugh, P., *Defining the Situation: The Organization of Meaning in Social Interaction*. Indianapolis: Bobbs-Merrill, 1968.

_____ A Common-Sense Conception of Deviance. In J. D. Douglas (ed.), *Deviance and Respectability. The Social Construction of Moral Meanings*. New York: Basic Books, 1970, pp. 61-88.

Mead, M., *Sex and Temperament in Three Primitive Societies*. New York: Wm. Morrow, 1935.

_____ *From the South Seas*. New York: Wm. Morrow, 1939.

_____ *Coming of Age in Samoa*. New York: Wm. Morrow, 1949.

_____ *Culture and Commitment. A Study of the Generation Gap*. Garden City, N. Y.: published for the Amer. Museum of Nat. History, Natural History Press, 1970.

_____ *Blackberry Winter*. New York: Wm. Morrow, 1972.

Mednick, S., Factors Related to Breakdown in Children at High Risk for Schizophrenia. In M. Roff and D. F. Richs (eds.), *Life History Research in Psychopathology*. Minneapolis: University of Minnesota Press, 1970.

Meggitt, M. J., *Desert People*. Sydney: Angus and Robertson, 1962.

Mills, C. W., Situated Action and the Vocabulary of
    Motives. *American Sociological Review*. 6: 904-
    913, 1940.
_____ *The Sociological Imagination*. New York:
    Oxford University Press, 1950.
Moore, S. F., Legal Liability and Evolutionary Interpre-
    tation: Some Aspects of Strict Liability, Self-Help,
    and Collective Responsibility. In, M. Gluckman (ed.),
    The Allocation of Responsibility. Manchester Univer-
    sity Press, 1972.
Moore, W., *Social Change*. Englewood Cliffs, N. J.:
    Prentice-Hall, 1963.
Morgan, H. W., *Yesterday's Addicts: American Society
    and Drug Abuse, 1825-1920*. Norman: University
    of Oklahoma Press, 1974.
Murphy, R. F., *The Dialectics of Social Life*. New
    York: Basic Books, 1972.
Naroll, R., and Cohen, R. (eds.), *A Handbook of Method
    in Cultural Anthropology*. New York: The Natural
    History Press, 1970.
Nash, J., Death as a Way of Life: The Increasing
    Resort to Homicide in a Maya Indian Community.
    American Anthropologist. 69: 455-470, 1967.
Newman, P. L., Wild Man Behavior in a New Guinea
    Highlands Community. *American Anthropologist*.
    66: 1-19, 1964.
Nisbet, R. A., *The Sociological Tradition*. New York:
    Basic Books, 1966.
O'Connor, G.; Wurmser, L.; Brown, T.; and Smith, J.,
    The Drug Addiction Business. *Drug Forum*. 1: 3-12,
    1971.
Oliver, S. C., Individuality, Freedom of Choice, and
    Cultural Flexibility of the Kamba. *American
    Anthropologist*. 67: 421-428, 1965.
Opler, M. E., The Human Being in Culture Theory.
    American Anthropologist. 66: 507-528, 1964.
Parker, S., The Witiko Psychosis in the Context of
    Ojibwa Personality and Culture. *American Anthro-
    pologist*. 62: 603-623, 1960.
Pastore, N., *The Nature-Nurture Controversy*. New York:
    King's Crown Press, 1949.
Payne, R., *The Life and Death of Adolph Hitler*. New
    York: Popular Library, 1973.

Peters, R. S., *The Concept of Motivation*. London: Routledge and Kegan Paul, 1958.

Piddington, R., Malinowski's Theory of Needs. In R. Firth (ed.), *Man and Culture*. London: Routledge and Kegan Paul, 1957.

Pirenne, H., *Medieval Cities*. New York: Doubleday, 1956.

Pospisil, L., Social Change and Primitive Law: Consequences of a Papuan Legal Case. *American Anthropologist*. 60: 832-837, 1958.

Premack, D., Language in Chimpanzee? *Science*. 172: 808-822, 1971.

Radcliffe-Brown, A. R., *The Andaman Islanders: A Study in Social Anthropology*. Cambridge University Press, 1922.

Radhakrishnan, S., and Raju, P. T. (eds.), *The Concept of Man*. Lincoln, Nebraska: Johnson Publishing Co., 1972.

Radin, P., *Primitive Man as Philosopher*. New York: D. Appleton, 1927.

Rasmussen, K., *Across Arctic America*. New York: G. P. Putnam Sons, 1927.

Redfield, R., The Folk Society. *American Journal of Sociology*. 52: 293-308, 1947.

_____ *The Little Community. Viewpoints for the Study of a Human Whole*. Chicago: University of Chicago Press, 1955.

Reichel-Dolmatoff, G., and Reichel-Dolmatoff, A., *The People of Aritama: The Cultural Personality of a Columbian Mestizo Village*. London: Routledge and Kegan Paul, 1961.

Rimland, B., Psychogenesis versus Biogenesis: The Issues and the Evidence. In S. Plog and R. Edgerton (eds.), *Changing Perspectives in Mental Illness*. New York: Holt, Rinehart and Winston, 1969, pp. 702-735.

Romney, K., and Romney, R., The Mixtecans of Juxtlahuaca, Mexico. In B. B. Whiting (ed.), *Six Cultures: Studies of Child Rearing*. New York: Wiley, 1963.

Rosenhan, D. L., On Being Sane in Insane Places. *Science*. 179: 250-258, 1973.

Rosenthal, D., *Genetic Theory of Abnormal Behavior*.
New York: McGraw-Hill, 1970
_____ *Genetics of Psychopathology*. New York:
McGraw-Hill, 1971.
Sartre, J. P., *Saint Genet*. New York: New American
Library, 1964.
Scheffler, H., *Choiseul Island Social Structure*.
Berkeley: University of California Press, 1965.
Schur, E. M., *Labeling Deviant Behavior. Its Socio-
logical Consequences*. New York: Harper & Row,
1971.
Scott, M. B., and Lyman, S. M., Accounts. *American
Sociological Review*. 33: 46-61, 1968.
Selby, H., *Zapotec Deviance: The Convergence of Folk
and Modern Sociology*. Austin, Texas: University of
Texas Press, 1974.
Singer, M., A Survey of Culture and Personality
Theory and Research. In Bert Kaplan (ed.), *Studying
Personality Cross-Culturally*. New York: Harper
& Row, 1961, pp. 9-90.
Skinner, A. B , Notes on the Eastern Cree and North-
ern Saulteaux. *Anthropological Papers of the
American Museum of Natural History*, 9, (Part I),
1912, pp. 1-177.
Slater, E., and Cowie, V., *The Genetics of Mental
Disorders*. London: Oxford University Press, 1971.
Smith, W., and Roberts, J., *Zuñi Law, a Field of Values*.
Cambridge, Massachusetts: Papers of the Peabody
Museum, Vol. 43, No. 1, 1954.
Spencer, P., *The Samburu*. Berkeley: University of
California Press, 1965.
Sperry, R., Mind, Brain and Humanist Values. In, J.
Platt (ed.), *New Views on Human Nature*. Chicago:
University of Chicago Press, 1965, pp. 71-92.
Spiro, M. E., Human Nature in its Psychological
Dimensions. *American Anthropologist*. 56: 19-30,
1954.
Stanner, W. E. H., Continuity and Schism in an Afri-
can Tribe. *Oceania*. 29: 208-217, 1959.
Stayton, D.; Hogan, R.; and Ainsworth, M. D. S.,
Infant Obedience and Maternal Behavior: The
Origins of Socialization Reconsidered. *Child
Development*. 42: 1057-1069, 1971.

Stevenson, L., *Seven Theories of Human Nature*. Oxford: The Clarendon Press, 1974.

Sudnow, D. (ed.), *Studies in Social Interaction*. New York: The Free Press, 1972.

Sutherland, E. H., and Cressey, D. R., *Principles of Criminology*, 6th ed. Chicago: Lippincott, 1960.

Talayesva, D. D., and Simmons, L. W., (eds.), *Sun Chief The Autobiography of a Hopi Indian*. New Haven, Conn.: Yale University Press, 1942.

Thomas, A.; Chess, S.; and Birch, H., *Temperament and Behavior Disorders in Children*. New York: Holt, Rinehart and Winston, 1968.

Thomas, E. M., *The Harmless People*. New York: Random House, 1958.

Tiger, L., *Men in Groups*. New York: Random House, 1969.

Tiger, L., and Fox, R., *The Imperial Animal*. New York: Holt, Rinehart and Winston, 1971.

Turnbull, C. M., *The Forest People*. New York: Simon and Schuster, 1961.

_____ *The Wayward Servants; the Two Worlds of the African Pygmies*. Garden City, New York: Natural History Press, 1965.

_____ *The Mountain People*. New York: Simon and Schuster, 1972.

Valenstein, E., *Brain Control*. New York: John Wiley & Sons, 1973.

Vandenberg, S. G. (ed.), *Progress in Human Behavior Genetics*. Baltimore: The Johns Hopkins Press, 1968.

Wallace, A. F. C., Anthropological Contributions to the Theory of Personality. In E. Norbeck, *et al.*, (eds.), *The Study of Personality*. New York: Holt, Rinehart and Winston, 1967.

_____ Mental Illness, Biology and Culture. In F. L. K. Hsu (ed.), *Psychological Anthropology.*, New Edition. Cambridge, Massachusetts: Schenkman, 1972.

Washburn, S. L., and Lancaster, C. S., The Evolution of Hungtin. In S. L. Washburn and P. C. Jay (eds.), *Perspectives on Human Evolution*. New York: Holt, Rinehart and Winston, 1968.

Watson, J. B., *Behaviorism*. Chicago: University of
Chicago Press, 1925.
Werner, E. E.; Bierman, J. M.; and French, F. E., *The
Children of Kauai*. Honolulu: University of Hawaii
Press, 1971.
Westman, J. C. (ed.), *Individual Differences in Chil-
dren*. New York: John Wiley & Sons, 1973.
Weyer, E. M., *The Eskimos*. New Haven: Yale University
Press, 1924.
White, M., and White, L., *The Intellectual Versus the
City*. Cambridge: Harvard University Press, 1962.
Wiele, E. F., On Social Psychological Questions in
Suicidal Personalities. *Psychological Research*.
11: 37-44,
Willems, E., Peasantry and City: Cultural Persistence
and Change in Historical Perspective, a European
Case. *American Anthropologist*. 72: 528-544, 1970.
Williams, R. J., *Biochemical Individuality*. New York:
John Wiley & Sons, 1956.
Windle, W. F., Brain Damage by Asphyxia at Birth.
Scientific American. 216: 77-84, 1969.
Winter, E. H., *Beyond the Mountains of the Moon*.
London: Routledge and Kegan Paul, 1959.
Wrong, D., The Oversocialized Conception of Man in
Modern Sociology. *American Sociological Review*.
26: 183-193, 1961.
Zamenhof, S., DNA (cell no.) and Protein in Neonatal
Rat Brain: Alteration by Timing of Maternal Dietary
Protein Restriction. *Journal of Nutrition*. 101:
1265-1269, 1971.
Zigler, E., The Nature-Nurture Issue Reconsidered. In,
H. C. Haywood (ed.), *Social-Cultural Aspects of
Mental Retardation*. New York: Appleton-Century-
Crofts, 1970, pp. 81-106.

AUTHOR INDEX

Abelson, R., 98
Ammar, H., 61
Arensberg, C., 54, 55
Ashley-Montagu, M., 91
Austin, J., 29

Bailey, F., 107
Bandura, A., 22
Baroja, J., 13
Bateson, G., 99
Beals, A., 69
Becker, E., 91
Becker, H., 14, 23
Belo, J., 15
Benedict, R., 9, 11, 15, 16, 85
Bennett, J., 16
Benthall, J., 94
Berlyne, B., 99
Birch, H., 23, 83, 88, 89
Block, M., 72
Blum, A., 29
Blum, R., 56
Blythe, R., 69
Bohannan, P., 42
Bowen, E., 34
Briggs, J., 62

Brown, J., 100
Bruner, E., 72, 73
Burke, K., 29
Burrows, E., 43

Callan, H., 93
Carstairs, G., 58
Castaneda, C., 57
Chagnon, N., 44
Chapple, E., 87
Chess, S., 23, 88, 89
Chomsky, N., 95
Cloward, R., 21
Cohen, A., 11, 18, 22, 25, 105
Cohen, R., 33
Cohen, Y., 52
Colson, E., 109
Conant, F., 48
Cooley, C., 14
Cowie, V., 23, 82
Cravioto, J., 83
Cressey, D., 21

D'Aquili, E., 90, 95
de Coulanges, F., 13
Devereux, G., 11, 41

SUBJECT INDEX